Ten

GW00362764

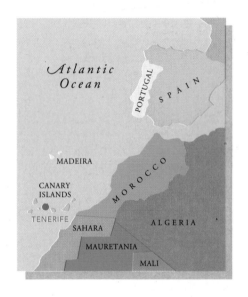

Atlantic Ocean

PORTUGAL

SPAIN

MADEIRA

MOROCCO

CANARY ISLANDS

TENERIFE

SAHARA

ALGERIA

MAURETANIA

MALI

DIAMOND BOOKS

Los Roques, Parque Nacional del Teide

YOUR COLLINS TRAVELLER

**Your Collins Traveller Guide will help you find your way around
your chosen destination quickly and easily. It is colour-coded for
easy reference:**

The blue section answers the question 'I would like to see or do something; where do I go and what do I see when I get there?' This section is
arranged as an alphabetical list of topics and it is recommended that an
up-to-date atlas or street plan is used in conjunction with the location
maps. Within each topic you will find:
- A selection of the best examples on offer.
- How to get there, costs and opening hours for each entry.
- The outstanding features of each entry.
- A simplified map, with each entry plotted and the nearest landmark
  or transport access.

The red section is a lively and informative gazetteer. It offers:
- Essential facts about the main places and cultural items.
  What is La Bastille? Who was Michelangelo? Where is Delphi?

The gold section is full of practical and invaluable travel information.
It offers:
- Everything you need to know to help you enjoy yourself and get the
  most out of your time away, from Accommodation through
  Baby-sitters, Car Hire, Food, Health, Money, Newspapers, Taxis,
  Telephones to Youth Hostels.

Cross-references:

Type in small capitals – **CHURCHES** – tells you that more information on an item is available within the topic on churches.

A-Z after an item tells you that more information is available
within the gazetteer. Simply look under the appropriate name.

A name in bold – **Holy Cathedral** – also tells you that more information on an item is available in the gazetteer – again simply
look up the name.

CONTENTS

CONTENTS

■ PRACTICAL INFORMATION GAZETTEER

Playa de las Teresitas

INTRODUCTION

If there's one thing better than a summer holiday in Tenerife, it's a winter holiday there. Just a few hours after shedding warm woollies and wrenching yourself away from subzero temperatures, you step off the aircraft not only in another continent but in a different climate. It's a place for all seasons – and all of them are warm and welcoming. If you have no desire to return home bronzed, or sit at a seaside café at midnight wearing only shorts and T-shirt, this is not the place for you. The temperature in winter 'falls' to 18°C. Little wonder that the Canary Islands are also referred to as the Fortunate Islands.

To a large extent, they have made their own fortune. The islands were born out of subsea volcanic eruptions so the land is barren rock and dust. However, around the resorts a lot of hard work has gone into creating floral explosions of colour. Soil was imported, an intricate irrigation system set up, and plants which have pride of place in pots on window ledges in Britain grow wild in Tenerife as hedgerows. A stroll along the quiet backstreets is like walking through the most carefully cultivated of hothouses.

The other major attraction of Tenerife is that it is a duty-free island. The regional government of the Canary Islands recognizes the earning potential of alcohol and tobacco, and is dedicated to keeping costs down. This was a major factor in its refusal to become a fully integrated part of the Common Market. Locally-produced spirits cost about £3 per litre, and cigarettes and excellent cigars can be purchased for pennies.

A word of warning: there the bargains end. The shops are crammed with cameras, watches, hi-fis and high-tech gadgetry. The covers and cases carry the names of reputable manufacturers but many are fakes, made in Far East countries. Examine the guarantee to discover the country of origin. Lace and leather goods are also plentiful but prices vary from shop to shop. By all means express an interest with a trader but look at what others are charging. Bartering is not welcomed but prices can be reduced instantly by about 10%.

Hotels on the island are superb. Bedrooms are clean and spacious, swimming pools exciting and immaculately kept, and owners compete fiercely to create the most attractive reception areas and bars. The major emphasis is on marble, ponds and waterfalls, with many hotels proudly displaying plaques proclaiming the company which created the interior

design. What's the food like? Britons and Germans form a large percentage of tourists, so food is prepared to their tastes. There is also an appetizing selection of local dishes, each of which is delightful to the palate.

Apartments on the island are plentiful and pleasant, if functional, and most have their own swimming pools. The regional government of the island has decreed that the building of new hotels and apartments must be completed in a few years' time. This means, however, that a plethora of earth movers, diggers and shovellers is gouging huge holes into volcanic craters to prepare foundations. Acres of rock and dust are being transformed into a giant Legoland, with grey blocks sprouting where only cacti could survive. You could do worse than seek assurances from your travel agent or tour operator that the beautiful accommodation shown in the glossy brochure is not in fact next door to a building site.

Tenerife is dominated by Mount Teide, the 3717 m volcano in the centre of the island. Even in summer its peak, the highest on Spanish land, is snow-capped. A cable car will take you close to the summit, and the fittest and keenest can brave the climb in thin air to the top. From there, you can see the other islands in the Canaries and, it is said, a clear day reveals the coast of Africa. However, it is also said that the celebrated dragon tree in Icod de los Vinos, a town at Teide's toes, is 3500 years old. How do they know? A tourist guide confided, 'It might be 350 years old. But 3500 years is better, yes?'

There is a variety of trips and excursions available for the adventurer. The more energetic should take advantage of the water sports, including paragliding, windsurfing, water-skiing and surfing. Then again, there is the sun and hundreds of delightful cafés. A final word of caution: it is easy and tempting to overindulge in amber rays or liquid. The results of both are painful. So relax and enjoy your stay!

William Coffey

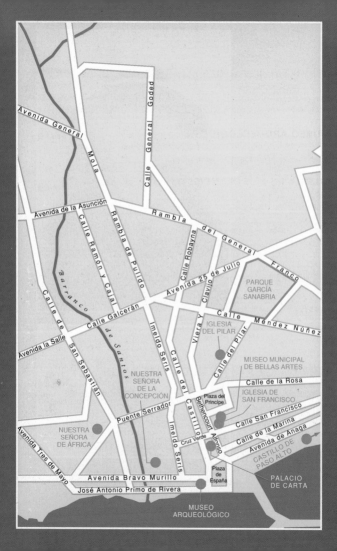

Santa Cruz

MUSEO MUNICIPAL DE BELLAS ARTES c/ José Murphy 4.
■ 1000-2000 Mon.-Fri.
Fine collection of paintings and sculpture. Displays the work of Canarian artists as well as Brueghel, Ribera, Jordaens, Van Loo, etc. See **WALK 1**.

MUSEO ARQUEOLÓGICO Palacio Insular, c/ Bravo Murillo.
■ 0900-1300, 1600-1800 Mon.-Fri., 0900-1300 Sat. ● 200 ptas.
Guanche (see **A-Z**) *artefacts, ceramics, mummies, etc. See* **WALK 1**.

IGLESIA DE SAN FRANCISCO Plaza de San Francisco.
■ According to Masses.
Late-17thC Franciscan chapel with fine Baroque sculptures. See **WALK 1**.

IGLESIA DEL PILAR c/ del Pilar.
■ According to Masses.
18thC church with a beautiful painted ceiling. See **WALK 1**.

PALACIO DE CARTA Plaza de la Candelaria 8.
■ 0900-1400 Mon.-Fri.
Splendid Canarian interior patio with tropical plants. See **WALK 1**, **A-Z**.

CASTILLO DE PASO ALTO Avenida Anaga.
■ Contact tourist office for open times. Taxi, bus from Plaza de España.
Castle which has been converted into a military museum. See **Nelson**.

NUESTRA SEÑORA DE ÁFRICA c/ San Sebastián.
■ 0630-1300 Mon.-Sat.
The city's main market, housed in an enormous renovated building.

PARQUE GARCÍA SANABRIA West of the city near c/ del Pilar.
■ Unrestricted access.
The municipal park, with a jumble of rare tropical plants. See **WALK 1**.

NUESTRA SEÑORA DE LA CONCEPCIÓN Plaza de la Iglesia.
■ 0730-1000, 1230-1300, 1700-2030.
18thC Baroque church with magnificent sculpted altar. See **WALK 1**, **A-Z**.

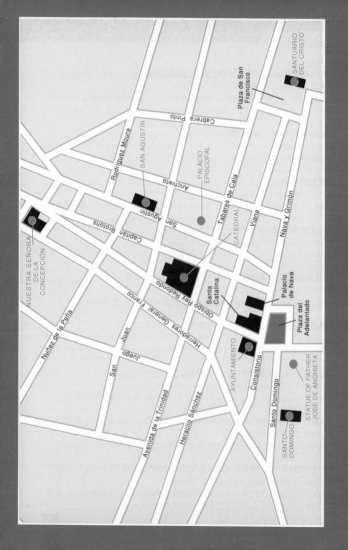

SANTUARIO
DEL CRISTO

Plaza de San
Francisco

Cabrera Pinto

Rodríguez Moure

SAN AGUSTÍN

San Agustín

Anchieta

PALACIO
EPISCOPAL

Tabares de Cala

Viana

CATEDRAL

Nava y Grimón

Capitán Brotons

NUESTRA SEÑORA
DE LA
CONCEPCIÓN

Obispo Rey Redondo

Santa Catalina

Palacio
de Nava

Herradores General Franco

Núñez de la Peña

San Juan

Juego

Plaza del
Adelantado

AYUNTAMIENTO

Consistorio

Avenida de la Trinidad

Heraclio Sánchez

Santo Domingo

STATUE OF FATHER
JOSE DE ANCHIETA

SANTO
DOMINGO

CATEDRAL Plaza de la Catedral.
■ 0800-1000, 1700-2030 and according to Masses.
Has a neoclassical façade and houses many treasures. See WALK 2, **A-Z**.

NUESTRA SEÑORA DE LA CONCEPCIÓN
Plaza de la Concepción. ■ According to Masses.
Founded in 1497 and the oldest of Tenerife's churches. See WALK 2, **A-Z**.

AYUNTAMIENTO (Town Hall), Plaza del Adelantado.
■ 0900-1300.
19thC building beautifully restored in typical Canarian style. See WALK 2.

SANTO DOMINGO Plaza de Santo Domingo 1.
■ Contact town hall for opening times.
See the beautiful dragon tree (see **Drago***) in the monastery gardens and admire the frescoes housed in this 16th-17thC early Renaissance-style church. See* WALK 2.

SAN AGUSTÍN c/ San Agustín.
■ 0830-early evening Mon.-Fri., 0830-1300 Sat.
Walk round the beautiful inner cloister of this former 17thC monastery, largely destroyed by fire at the beginning of this century. See WALK 2.

SANTUARIO DEL CRISTO Plaza de San Francisco.
■ Contact town hall for opening times.
One of the island's most venerated images, the Santísimo Cristo de la Laguna (see **A-Z***), is kept in this former Franciscan chapel. See* WALK 2.

PALACIO EPISCOPAL c/ San Agustín.
■ Interior closed to the public.
Elegant 17thC Baroque palace built by the counts of Salazar.

STATUE OF FATHER JOSÉ DE ANCHIETA On the round-about at the entrance to the town, opposite the university buildings.
A bronze sculpture by Bruno Giggi (1959) donated by the Brazilian government in honour of this missionary who came from La Laguna.

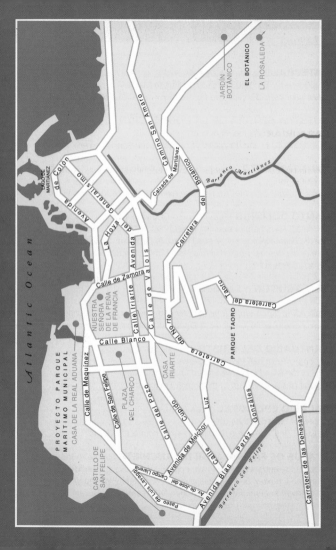

NUESTRA SEÑORA DE LA PEÑA DE FRANCIA
Plaza de la Iglesia. ■ Open according to Masses.
Much-altered façade but inside are examples of the work of the Canarian artist Luis de la Cruz and the sculptor Luján Pérez. See **WALK 3**.

CASA IRIARTE c/ San Juan.
■ 0900-1300, 1600-1900 Mon.-Fri., 0900-1300 Sat.
An 18thC mansion boasting fine carved balconies and a pretty patio. It now houses craft studios, shops, a naval museum and an interesting display of historical photographs of the area. See **SHOPPING 2**, **WALK 3**.

CASTILLO DE SAN FELIPE Paseo de Luis Lavaggi.
■ Interior closed to the public. Free bus from Plaza Martiánez.
An 18thC castle of interest for its Spanish colonial-style façade, which has the coat of arms of Philip IV of Spain. Set in an attractive garden.

PLAZA DEL CHARCO At the foot of c/ Blanco.
The focal point of the town, with imported Indian laurel trees and a children's playground. Stop here and watch the world go by. See **WALK 3**.

CASA DE LA REAL ADUANA c/ Lonjas.
■ 0930-1300, 1600-1900 Mon.-Fri., 0930-1300 Sat.
The oldest surviving building in Puerto de la Cruz, dating from 1620, and formerly a customs house. The inner patio now houses craft and souvenir shops. See **SHOPPING 2**, **WALK 3**.

LA ROSALEDA c/ Camino Lazo.
■ 0900-1800. Free bus from Plaza Martiánez. ● 700 ptas.
Some 10,000 roses form the centrepiece of these exotic gardens. There are also giant water lilies, tropical birds and free wine-tasting.

JARDÍN BOTÁNICO Ctra del Botánico.
■ 0900-1900 summer, 0900-1800 winter. ● 100 ptas.
A marvellous display of plants, both indigenous to the Canary Islands and from all over the world. Created in the late 18thC, the gardens demonstrate the benefits of the local climate. See **A-Z**.

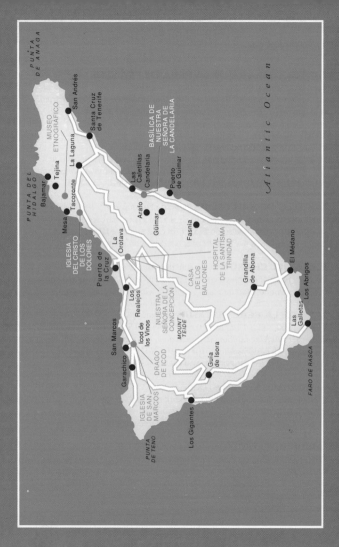

BASÍLICA DE NUESTRA SEÑORA DE LA CANDELARIA

Avenida Litoral, Candelaria.

■ 0730-1300, 1500-2030 (winter till 1930), and according to Masses.

Built near the seafront in 1958 to house the replica of the famous Virgen de la Candelaria. See **Nuestra Señora de la Candelaria**.

DRAGO DE ICOD c/ Hércules, Icod de los Vinos.

Magnificent dragon tree, perhaps 3500 years old. See EXCURSION 1, **A-Z**.

NUESTRA SEÑORA DE LA CONCEPCIÓN

Plaza Casanas, La Orotava. ■ According to Masses.

Baroque façade housing splendid high altarpiece. See EXCURSION 1, **A-Z**.

CASA DE LOS BALCONES c/ San Francisco, La Orotava.

■ 0900-1300, 1600-1930 Mon.-Fri., 0900-1300 Sat.

17thC building with beautiful carved wooden balconies. Visit the patio and watch girls in national costume doing embroidery work. See EXCURSION 1.

HOSPITAL DE LA SANTÍSIMA TRINIDAD Plaza San

Francisco, La Orotava. ■ 1030-1200 Sun. & hols, 1600-1730 daily.

Former monastery with fine views of Orotava valley. See EXCURSION 1.

IGLESIA DEL CRISTO DE LOS DOLORES

Plaza de San Agustín, Tacoronte. ■ According to Masses.

Houses a revered 17thC statue of Christ. See EXCURSION 3, **A-Z**.

MUSEO ETNOGRÁFICO Ctra Tacoronte, Valle de Guerra.

■ 1000-1300, 1600-1900. ● 200 ptas.

A pleasing display of crafts, tools and 'life as it used to be'. See EXCURSION 3.

IGLESIA DE SAN MARCOS Plaza de la Iglesia, Icod de los

Vinos. ■ According to Masses.

A Renaissance-style church with a painted wooden ceiling. See EXCURSION 1.

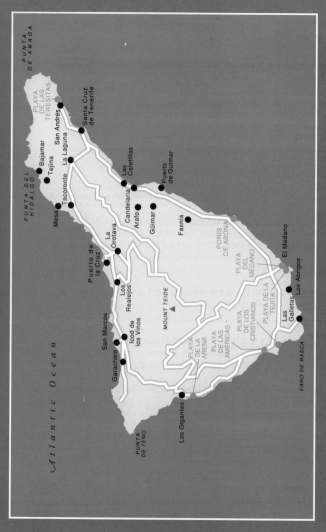

PLAYA DE LAS TERESITAS 9 km northeast of Santa Cruz.
San Andrés bus from Avenida Anaga, Santa Cruz.
Impressive artificial beach of golden sand. Calm bay protected by stone dyke and palm trees. Often quiet in the week. See **EXCURSION 3**.

PORIS DE ABONA 41 km southwest of Santa Cruz.
Bus 118, 130.
Medium-sized bay of fine black sand. No facilities, and often crowded at weekends with families from Santa Cruz.

PLAYA DEL MÉDANO 60 km southwest of Santa Cruz.
Bus 116, 117 from Santa Cruz, Bus 342 from Puerto de la Cruz.
Resort with long stretch of yellow sand, near Reina Sofía airport. Shallow water and exposed to the wind, so it's popular for surfing.

PLAYA DE LA TEJITA 3 km southwest of El Médano.
Access via Playa del Médano.
A good sheltered beach on the south coast, set beneath the small rocky outcrop of Montaña Roja.

PLAYA DE LOS CRISTIANOS 75 km southwest of Santa Cruz.
Bus 111 from Santa Cruz.
Stretches of soft, brown sand protected by jetties, near the ferry port of this resort. Beach equipment for hire. Water sports. Safe for children.

PLAYA DE LAS AMÉRICAS 3 km northwest of Los Cristianos.
Bus 111 from Santa Cruz.
Varied beaches with hard sand, grainy sand, pebbles and rocks strung along the tree-lined promenade. All water-sports equipment available for hire. See **EXCURSION 1**, **A-Z**.

PLAYA DE LA ARENA 30 km northwest of Los Cristianos.
Access from Puerto de Santiago.
A bay of fine, black sand, steeply sloping underwater, with rocks to either side. Overlooked by a terraced restaurant and with good views of Gomera (see **A-Z**). *See* **EXCURSION 1**.

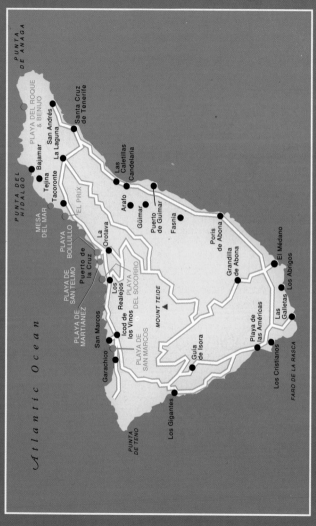

PLAYA DEL ROQUE & BENIJO 2-4 km northeast of Taganana.
Scenic beaches with big waves and a strong undertow, so don't swim too far. There are a number of beach restaurants. See **EXCURSION 3**.

MESA DEL MAR 7 km north of Tacoronte.
Take the TF 122 from Tacoronte and turn left after 4 km.
A recent tourist development on the rugged northern coastline, offering a good, small beach of black sand set beneath steep cliffs.

EL PRIX 8 km north of Tacoronte, next to Mesa del Mar.
Take the TF 122 from Tacoronte and turn left after 4 km.
Charming fishing port with a small beach of fine, black sand and good restaurants but no amenities. A favourite with the locals.

PLAYA BOLLULLO On the beach road north of Puerto de la Cruz.
30 min walk from centre of Puerto de la Cruz.
Lovely, secluded little beach for those seeking peace and quiet. Lacking in amenities but good for swimming.

PLAYA DE MARTIÁNEZ Avenida de Colón, Puerto de la Cruz.
A small bay of black sand with a rock jetty providing protection from the waves and wind, and with restaurants nearby.

PLAYA DE SAN TELMO c/ de San Telmo, Puerto de la Cruz.
Not a beach as such but fun to look down on and watch the waves break dramatically over the rocky promontory. See **WALK 3**.

PLAYA DEL SOCORRO 8 km west of Puerto de la Cruz.
Take the C 820 from Puerto de la Cruz and turn off at Los Realejos.
Isolated beach with tapas huts (see **Food***) and a shower formed by a cascading freshwater spring. Currents can make swimming treacherous.*

PLAYA DE SAN MARCOS 24 km west of Puerto de la Cruz.
Take the C 820 from Puerto de la Cruz and turn off at Icod de los Vinos.
Medium-sized bay of dark, fine sand and clear water, surrounded by rugged cliffs offering beautiful views over the sea. See **EXCURSION 1**.

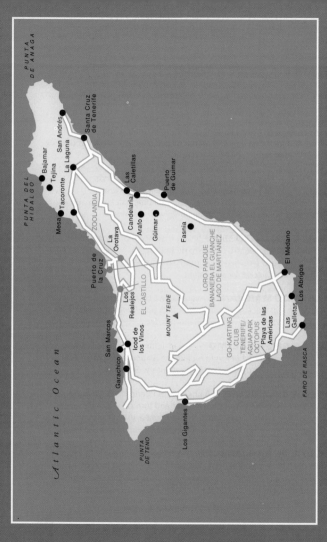

LORO PARQUE c/ San Felipe, Punta Brava. ■ 0830-1800. Free bus from Plaza Martiánez, Puerto de la Cruz. ● 1400 ptas.
Over 1300 parrots in a beautiful tropical setting with spectacular shows throughout the day. Trained parrots, dolphins and other animals too.

BANANERA EL GUANCHE Villa de la Orotova, Puerto de la Cruz. ■ 0900-1800. Free bus from Plaza Martiánez. ● 700 ptas.
*Tour a real banana plantation (see **A-Z**) and see dozens of other exotic plants. Good for older children. Mum and dad get a free banana liqueur.*

LAGO DE MARTIÁNEZ Playa de Martiánez, Puerto de la Cruz. ■ 0900-1800. ● 300 ptas.
Beautifully designed seaside lido, where the kids can splash in the pools and fountains while the adults concentrate on getting a tan.

GO-KARTING CLUB TENERIFE Ctra General, Playa de las Américas. On the road to Reina Sofía airport.
■ 0900-1800. ● 1000-1500 ptas.
Low-down fun – quick or slow – for adults and children. Five laps on a fast or slow kart for dad and 10 laps for the kids.

ZOOLANDIA c/ El Ramal, La Orotava. ■ 0900-1800. Free bus from Plaza Martiánez, Puerto de la Cruz. ● 800 ptas.
A subtropical garden is the setting for a zoo containing flora and fauna, both from the Canary Islands and well beyond, including lions, tigers, bears and apes.

AGUAPARK OCTOPUS San Eugenio, Playa de las Américas. ■ 1000-1800. ● 1500 ptas.
Water slides, water tunnels, a wave pool and a magical 'tap in the sky' are some of the attractions at the island's popular water park.

EL CASTILLO Ctra General del Norte, Los Realejos. 6 km from Puerto de la Cruz. ■ 0900-1800. ● 600 ptas.
A museum and park set in and around a real castle, including a farm, cactus garden and wine-tasting.

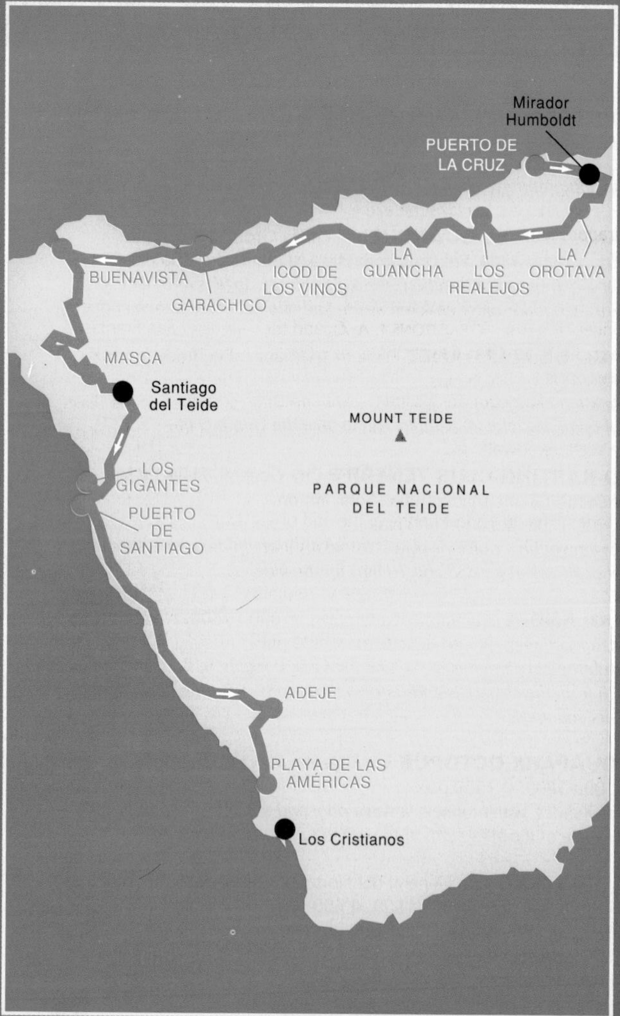
Mirador
Humboldt
PUERTO DE
LA CRUZ
LA
OROTAVA
LOS
REALEJOS
LA
GUANCHA
ICOD DE
LOS VINOS
GARACHICO
BUENAVISTA
MASCA
Santiago
del Teide
MOUNT TEIDE
PARQUE NACIONAL
DEL TEIDE
LOS
GIGANTES
PUERTO
DE
SANTIAGO
ADEJE
PLAYA DE LAS
AMÉRICAS
Los Cristianos

EXCURSION 1

A one-day excursion exploring the area round La Orotava, Icod de los Vinos, Masca and Los Gigantes.

Leave Puerto de la Cruz following signs for the motorway to Santa Cruz and after about 3 km take the exit for La Orotava, climbing up near the Mirador Humboldt.

8 km – La Orotava (see **A-Z**). A sedate town and one of the oldest in Tenerife. Make your way up through the shops in the newer part of town, bearing right to pass the 18thC cathedral, Nuestra Señora de la Concepción (see **ATTRACTIONS 4**, **A-Z**), and then along c/ San Francisco, where you pass Casa de los Balcones with its embroidery school (see **ATTRACTIONS 4**). Arriving at Plaza San Francisco, enjoy the view over La Orotava valley from the Hospital de la Santísima Trinidad (see **ATTRACTIONS 4**). Continue up out of town to take the Los Realejos road through the scattered dwellings.

16 km – Los Realejos (see **A-Z**). Once two villages used as camps by the opposing forces of the Guanches (see **A-Z**) and conquistadores, and the site of Tenerife's last battle, at the end of the 15thC. Follow the signs for La Guancha on the TF 221, climbing through Tigaiga and Icod de Alto, with good views of the valley, before arriving at La Guancha itself, a typical Canarian village. Turn right to rejoin the C 280, then bear left towards Icod de los Vinos.

39 km – Icod de los Vinos (see **A-Z**). Bear right through the town until you see Playa de San Marcos (see **BEACHES 2**) signposted on the right, and turn left towards the impressive dragon tree known as the Drago de Icod (see **ATTRACTIONS 4**, **A-Z**), and the beautiful Iglesia de San Marcos nearby (see **ATTRACTIONS 4**). You may wish to stop for a typical Canarian lunch at Carmen (see **RESTAURANTS 3**). Continue past the dragon tree along the C 820. After 6 km, past San Juan del Reparo, turn right towards Garachico and wind your way down the hairpin bends, resisting the superb views until you reach Tanque, where it is safe to stop. Continue past Las Cruces and San Pedro de Daute.

54 km – Garachico (see **A-Z**). A pleasant town that was almost completely destroyed by the 1706 eruption of Volcán de Negro, and was rebuilt on a semicircular mass of cooled lava.

63 km – Buenavista (see **A-Z**). The most northwesterly village in

Drago de Icod

Tenerife. A calm place with beautiful views and a 16thC church, Virgen de los Remedios. Take the road opposite the petrol station, heading for El Palmar, and start climbing into the Teno massif region. The views along the Valle del Palmar are breathtaking and the island of Gomera (see **A-Z**) is visible off the coast. The road narrows after El Palmar.

76 km – Masca. A tiny village spread out at the top of a gorge and formerly known as the 'hidden village' due to its inaccessibility. Masca is now on the tourist trail but retains much of its original identity. Continue south, climbing out of the gorge. After 6 km stop at the layby to marvel at the wonderful views of the sea on the right and Mount Teide (see **A-Z**) on the left. Then the road drops down steeply into Santiago del Teide. Turn right along the C 820. The road continues to twist and turn, albeit less dramatically. Turn right at Tamaimo on the TF 1480 towards Los Gigantes.

92 km – Los Gigantes (see **A-Z**). Turn right down the town's one-way system and descend towards the pleasant marina. Stop to browse through the shops or admire the awesome serenity of the cliffs. On the way back out of town, just beyond the taxi rank, stop off for refreshment and savour the atmosphere of one of the resort's oldest establishments, the aptly-named Bamboo Bar. Continue out of town and turn right for the short journey to Puerto de Santiago.

94 km – Puerto de Santiago. A tasteful little resort with a small bay of black sand, Playa de la Arena (see **BEACHES 1**), overlooked by a restaurant. Rejoin the main road south by turning right 2 km out of the village and enjoy the less dramatic scenery of the west coast.

114 km – Adeje. An attractive little village, best known as the starting point of the walk down the Barranco del Infierno (see **A-Z**). On its main street is the 17th-18thC church, Iglesia de Santa Úrsula. Return to the C 822 main road and follow it towards Playa de las Américas (see **BEACHES 1**, **A-Z**), which marks the end of the excursion (121 km).

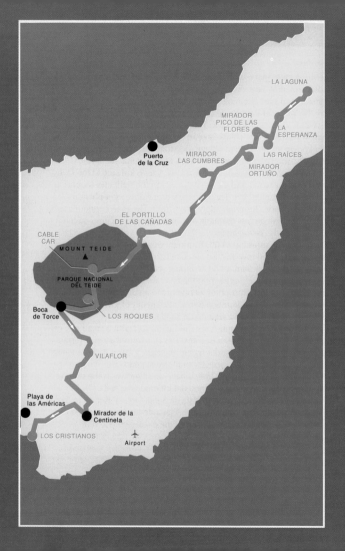

LA LAGUNA

MIRADOR
PICO DE LAS
FLORES

LA
ESPERANZA

MIRADOR
LAS CUMBRES

LAS RAÍCES

MIRADOR
ORTUÑO

Puerto
de la Cruz

EL PORTILLO
DE LAS CAÑADAS

CABLE
CAR

MOUNT TEIDE ▲

PARQUE NACIONAL
DEL TEIDE

Boca
de Torce

LOS ROQUES

VILAFLOR

Playa de
las Américas

Mirador de la
Centinela

LOS CRISTIANOS

✈
Airport

Mount Teide

A one-day excursion across Tenerife from Santa Cruz to Los Cristianos via Mount Teide.

Turn off the *autopista* from Santa Cruz at the signs for La Laguna university. Turn left at the first roundabout onto the C 824 which leads inland through gently undulating pasture land to the town of La Esperanza. The road begins to wind upwards along the spine of the island, with views of the sea off both coasts. Quite suddenly you enter Esperanza forest (see **A-Z**). Continue climbing through its magnificent greenery. Turn left after about 1 km, just in front of the Bar las Raíces café.

17 km – Las Raíces (see **A-Z**). A few hundred metres along the track there is a clearing among the tall pine trees, in the middle of which stands this historic monument. Return to the C 824.

20 km – Mirador Pico de las Flores. After a sharp bend to the right, you come to this mirador, with an impressive view over the southeasterly slopes, and a sighting of Santa Cruz in the distance. The road then straightens and levels out, and you'll find yourself driving through young silver eucalyptus trees and shrubs.

27 km – Mirador Ortuño. The mirador offers a splendid panorama of the northern coast and its resorts. Shortly afterwards you will catch glimpses, and then the full view, of Mount Teide. Take a detour to the right after 6 km along a small road leading to the Mirador las Cumbres.

35 km – Mirador las Cumbres. From here you can fully appreciate the snowcapped splendour of the mountain. Return to the C 824. At an altitude of 2000 m the forest ends, revealing a landscape of purple-brown earth dotted with *retama* (broom). Pass the Izaña meteorological station on the left.

54 km – El Portillo (see **Las Cañadas**). Turn left here, and on your right, shortly after the junction and set back slightly from the road, is the Centro de Visitantes (0900-1600 weather permitting), which covers the geology, history and biology of the Parque Nacional del Teide (see **A-Z**), with slides and specimens, and a video room running programmes in English (every hour on the half hour). Continue through this area's strange lunar landscape. Turn right after 11 km.

65 km – Mount Teide Cable Car. The cable car takes visitors (weather permitting) towards the peak of Mount Teide (see **WALK 4**, **A-Z**) and

there is also a restaurant offering expensive lunches. Back on the C 821, you pass the *parador* on the left (see **Accommodation**), and the turning on the right leads to the strange rock formations which are known as Los Roques.

69 km – Los Roques. From here there are extensive views of the crater below. As you continue towards the edge of the crater, notice the blue rock through which the road cuts, and the mysterious columns of rock which rise out of the crater wall. After about 7 km, bear left at the junction along the C 821. Once across the outer ridge, the landscape drops steeply away to the right as you descend through pine forests.

81 km – Vilaflor. At 1400 m, this is the highest village in Spain and is famous for the purity of its water. Set among neat terraced vineyards and almond trees, it offers peace and quiet and contains good examples of typical Canarian architecture. Follow the signs to Arona and Los Cristianos by turning right just outside the village. The road offers a panoramic view of the arid plains and volcanic outcrops of the south, with the airport to the left, and the beach resorts of Los Cristianos (see **A-Z**) and Playa de las Américas (see **A-Z**) behind the hills on the right.

Los Roques

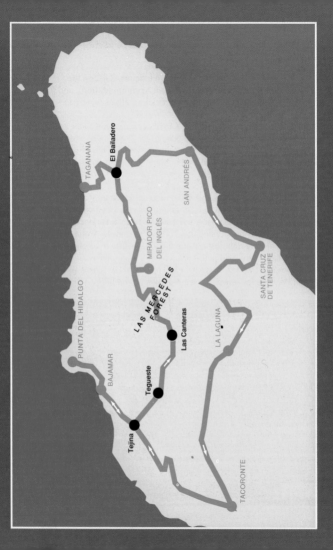

Anaga Mountains

A one-day excursion from Santa Cruz through the mountainous region at the northeastern tip of the island.

Take the *autopista* or the C 824 from Santa Cruz.

7 km – La Laguna (see **A-Z**). The university town of Tenerife and the island's first capital. Take time to wander through the town and appreciate the many fine examples of Canarian architecture, and stop to admire the Catedral (see **ATTRACTIONS 2, A-Z**) and Nuestra Señora de la Concepción (see **ATTRACTIONS 2, A-Z**). The C 820 out of town passes through Guamasa.

17 km – Tacoronte. Formerly a capital of the Guanches (see **A-Z**). Turn right to descend out of the town centre and notice the fine *drago* (see **A-Z**) on the right. The junction to the left of the tree takes you towards the older part of town where there are two fine examples of 16th and 17thC churches, Iglesia de Santa Catalina and Iglesia del Cristo de los Dolores (see **ATTRACTIONS 4, A-Z**). Return to the junction and take the Tejina road, the TF 122. Just outside Tacoronte look for a sign on the left for the Museo Etnográfico (Casa de Carta) (see **ATTRACTIONS 4**), and turn left down to the car park on the far side of the building. Continue through the banana plantations (see **A-Z**) of Valle de Guerra for 10 km to Tejina, where you should bear left at the roundabout.

30 km – Bajamar (see **A-Z**). A picturesque place and an ideal spot to have lunch. Turn left out of the resort.

33 km – Punta del Hidalgo. The road ends here at a roundabout, from where you can see the village's small, rocky beach and the rugged cliffs cutting into the sea. Return to the roundabout at Tejina (6 km) and turn left along the TF 121 which snakes up through eucalyptus and tamarisk trees to Tegueste. Continue for 4 km to Las Canteras, driving slowly in order to take a sharp U-turn to the left at the junction in the centre of the village, onto the TF 114.

48 km – Las Mercedes. Climb up into Las Mercedes forest through cedars and then laurel trees intermingled with briar. As you travel along the ridge which divides the island in two, both coasts become visible. Follow the signs for the Mirador Pico del Inglés.

55 km – Mirador Pico del Inglés. From here, at an altitude of 992 m, you can look down into the tree-clad Afur valley, often thinly veiled in a fine mist. Return from this 1 km detour and turn right to rejoin the road past Las Casas de la Cumbre. The road initially has a good surface and passing places, though it becomes narrower as you descend. At the foot (11 km) go straight on, following the signs for Taganana and San Andrés, and then turn left after 2 km to take the Taganana road, the TF 1124. The road takes you through a tunnel and round some steep hairpin bends.

72 km – Taganana. An extremely picturesque settlement (one of the oldest on the island), with the Roque de las Ánimas in the distance. It is worth continuing the 2 km on to Playa del Roque (see **BEACHES 2**) to swim or take refreshment in one of the roadside bars, or just to admire its romantic scenery. Return to Taganana (2 km) and turn left at the junction to take the San Andrés and Santa Cruz road, which affords good views of the cliffs and sea, again watching out for a series of sharp bends.

93 km – San Andrés. Here it is possible to take a short detour to the left and visit Tenerife's artificially created beach of golden sand, Playa de las Teresitas (see **BEACHES 1**), which has proved popular with the locals as well as holiday-makers. From here you can return to Santa Cruz along the TF 111 (102 km).

La Laguna

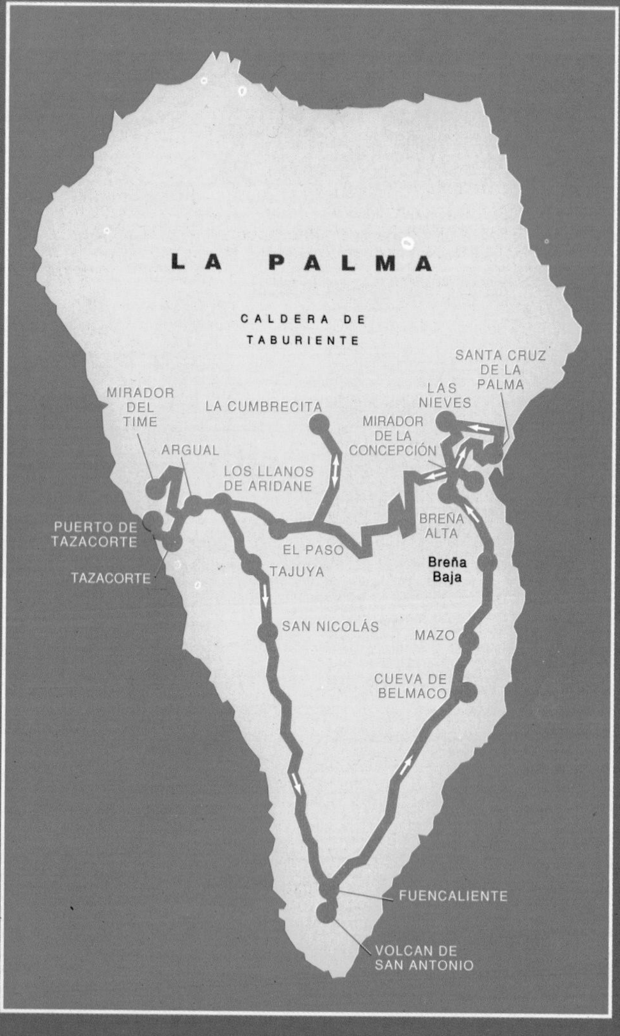

LA PALMA

CALDERA DE
TABURIENTE

SANTA CRUZ
DE LA
PALMA

LAS
NIEVES

MIRADOR
DEL
TIME

LA CUMBRECITA

MIRADOR
DE LA
CONCEPCIÓN

ARGUAL

LOS LLANOS
DE ARIDANE

BREÑA
ALTA

PUERTO DE
TAZACORTE

EL PASO

Breña
Baja

TAJUYA

TAZACORTE

SAN NICOLÁS

MAZO

CUEVA DE
BELMACO

FUENCALIENTE

VOLCAN DE
SAN ANTONIO

La Palma

A one-day excursion round the most fertile and one of the most beautiful of the Canary Islands. See **ISLANDS**, **A-Z**.

From Santa Cruz de la Palma take the road leading north and turn first left to climb steeply up from the coast.

5 km – Las Nieves. Built on the side of the mountain, this village church houses the jewelled 14thC statue of the island's patron saint, Nuestra Señora de las Nieves. Every five years La Bajada de la Virgen (The Descent of the Virgin) is celebrated, and the statue is carried to Santa Cruz de la Palma in a procession of floats representing miraculous inter-ventions of the saint. Continue south along the C 830, stopping after 5 km at the Mirador de la Concepción with its splendid view along the coast. Take the inland route, the TF 812, heading for El Paso. The road climbs the eastern slopes of the mountains before a tunnel provides access to the other side. Turn right 4 km after the tunnel.

34 km – La Cumbrecita. At 1833 m, this is a natural balcony which offers wonderful views of La Caldera de Taburiente, notably at the Mirador Lomo de las Chozas. The peaks of the ridge of this enormous crater can be seen opposite, and above rises the Roque de los Muchachos which, at 2426 m, is the highest point on the island. The monolithic rock called Idafe, which was an object of worship for the Guanches (see **A-Z**), can be seen rising from the floor of the crater. Retrace your route to the TF 812 and turn right through pine forests and almond groves.

46 km – El Paso. A centre of silk-making and for the local brand of cigars, Capote. The town is set among almond groves which attract numerous visitors when the trees blossom in Feb. Take the road to Los Llanos de Aridane past banana plantations (see **A-Z**).

50 km – Los Llanos de Aridane. The island's second town, an agricul-tural centre surrounded by banana plantations and almond groves. Take the C 832 across the valley and turn right at Argual. Every inch of the steep slopes has been used for banana cultivation. Note the irrigation channels clinging to the sides of the mountains.

61 km – Mirador del Time. This offers a panoramic view of the terraces of the valley of Aridane, the most beautiful valley on the island, and of the Barranco de las Angustias. At this point you should return to the

C 832 and turn right on the other side of the gorge, before Argual.

72 km – Tazacorte. A centre of banana cultivation. Visit La Casa de los Mártires, which commemorates the life of the Jesuit missionary, Father Azevedo, killed by Huguenot privateers on 15 July 1570. From Puerto de Tazacorte (3 km) you can take a 1 hr boat trip to the Cueva Bonita, an attractive cave with strange effects of blue light (approx. 1500 ptas). Puerto de Tazacorte is a popular resort with the locals and ideal for a lunch of fresh grilled fish. It is also of historical interest, for here the invading Spanish forces, led by Alonso Fernández de Lugo (see **A-Z**), landed in 1492. Return to Los Llanos de Aridane and take the C 832 towards the south of the island, past Tajuya and San Nicolás. The region was affected by a volcanic eruption in 1949 which divided the village of San Nicolás in two and left a startling legacy of lava fields.

101 km – Fuencaliente. This southernmost town is a wine-producing centre and here you can sample the finest *malvasía* (see **Drinks**) on the island. The town was a former hot-water spa until the source was destroyed by the 1677 eruption of the San Antonio volcano. Take a detour 1 km south to climb up to the craters (last active in 1971) and survey the surrounding countryside, still covered in ash yet already being cultivated. Take the C 832 through fields of lava and past a pine forest on the left. Fork right at Tigalate and drive along the fertile coastal strip with its steep cliffs.

115 km – Cueva de Belmaco. The dwelling place of the last native king of Tigalete. The significance of the cave lies in its prehistoric spiral inscriptions, which are as yet undeciphered but may turn out to be a form of writing.

119 km – Mazo. A charming village of whitewashed houses which line the steep streets and alleys. Beautiful 16thC statues of the Virgin are housed in the Iglesia de San Blas, behind which is an *atelier* where you can watch girls embroidering in the cool patio. Continue north along the winding road towards the village of Breña Baja, turning left to reach Breña Alta.

130 km – Breña Alta. Famous for its plaited palm work and as a source of mineral water. Just before entering the village, notice its twin *dragos* (see **A-Z**) on the left, in San Isidro. Follow signs for 11 km back into Santa Cruz de la Palma (141 km).

Casa de Colón, Gomera

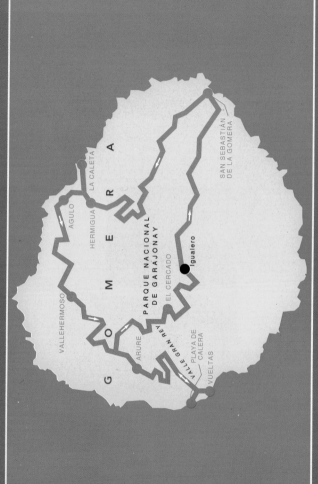

EXCURSION 5

Gomera

A one-day excursion round this small and lush island to the west of Tenerife. See **ISLANDS, A-Z**.

San Sebastián. The capital of the island and notable as a port of call for Christopher Columbus (see **A-Z**). He resided for a time in Casa de Colón in the town's charming main street. Visit the Torre del Conde, a 15thC fortified tower (and now a museum) where Beatriz de Bobadilla (see **A-Z**) took refuge from the rebellious Guanches (see **A-Z**). The Iglesia de la Asunción houses a 19thC fresco depicting the 1599 attack on Gomera by the Dutch. Leave the town by the main road northwest along the Barranco Seco (TF 711) to discover a pleasant countryside of terraces and orchards. Pass through the Túnel del Cumbre and arrive at the beautiful Valle de Hermigua. The road then descends towards the northern coast of the island.

23 km – Hermigua. The town is built on the slopes of the Barranco de Monteforte. Visit the two churches or swim at the pretty La Caleta beach east of the town, which has good views of Tenerife. From the beach it is possible to hire a boat to visit Los Órganos, impressive basalt columns which lie just north of Puerto de Vallehermoso.

27 km – Agulo. A village in a picturesque setting surrounded by high cliffs. Visit Los Telares, just before the village, and watch the women weaving.

42 km – Vallehermoso. An agricultural centre dominated by El Roque Cano, an imposing basalt rock formed by the erosion of the surrounding lava. Continue along the TF 711, winding through broom and pine forests, and then descend past the palm groves after Arure, offering splendid views over the canyon, and of the village of Taguluche to the right.

68 km – Valle Gran Rey. The most beautiful valley on the island, revealing different glimpses of scenery at each twist of the road. This is a majestic mountain countryside of terraced slopes and palm trees.

74 km – Vueltas. A small port at the foot of cliffs where you can have a leisurely seafood lunch. Boats leave here for Playa de Santiago. You might feel like a swim at the Playa de Calera, 2.5 km to the north. Return through Valle Gran Rey, then turn off to the right after about 18 km along the TF 713, between Arure and Vallehermosa. Take the

next right-hand fork to follow the road to Las Hayas and El Cercado.
97 km – El Cercado. The pottery made in this and other local villages is collectively known as Chipude, and in the workshops it is still possible to see potters at work. Continue for 1 km to Temocoda and then bear left and almost immediately right to take the road that leads to the outskirts of the Parque Nacional de Garajonay. At Igualero, 6 km on, take the turning to the left and after 1 km, at the following junction, take the road to the right and continue for 21 km back to San Sebastián (126 km).

San Sebastián

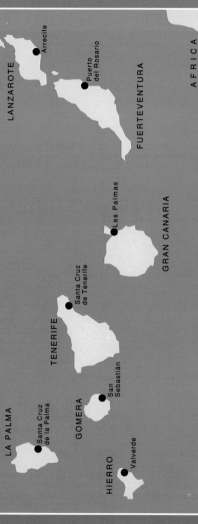

FUERTEVENTURA

Capital: Puerto del Rosario. Fuerteventura is only 90 km from the African coast and features African flora and sandy beaches. Frequent flights and ferries to Gran Canaria and Lanzarote. See **A-Z**.

GOMERA

Capital: San Sebastián. The only island with no recent volcanic activity. It possesses beautiful forests and picturesque hillsides. Daily ferry services to Tenerife. See **EXCURSION 5**, **A-Z**.

GRAN CANARIA

Capital: Las Palmas. The countryside is characterized by lush vegetation, gorges and volcanic areas. Regular flights and ferries to the other islands. See **A-Z**.

HIERRO

Capital: Valverde. The westernmost of the islands, and the smallest, Hierro is extremely beautiful and thus far unexploited by tourism. Regular flights to Tenerife and ferry services. See **A-Z**.

LANZAROTE

Capital: Arrecife. It retains the most recent effects of volcanic activity and features a strange but beautiful lunar landscape. Regular flights and ferry services to the other islands. See **A-Z**.

LA PALMA

Capital: Santa Cruz de la Palma. The island features one of the earth's biggest craters, the Caldera de Taburiente (800 m deep, 10 km wide). It is the most luxuriant of the Canary Islands. Regular flights and ferry services to the other islands. See **EXCURSION 4**, **A-Z**.

TENERIFE

Capital: Santa Cruz de Tenerife. The largest of the Canary Islands. The island has an extremely varied geography and climate. Daily flights to the Continent as well as numerous charter flights. Regular flights, and hydrofoil and ferry services, to the other islands. See **Orientation**.

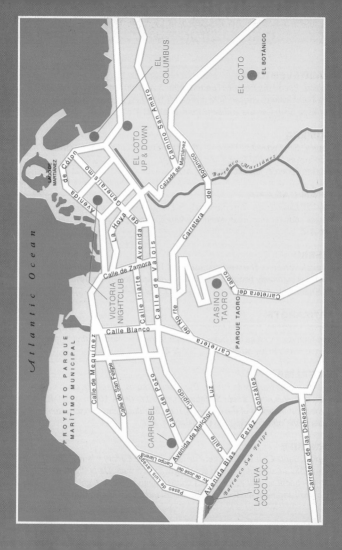

EL COTO UP & DOWN Oro Negro Hotel, Avenida de Colón 14.
■ 2200-0400. ● 3000 ptas.
A magnificent disco with up-market clientele.

LA CUEVA La Languera. 4 km west of Puerto de la Cruz.
■ 2000-0300. ● 4500 ptas.
Restaurant on a cliff with views over the sea. International entertainment in a Guanche (see A-Z) setting. African and flamenco dancing. See **Excursions**.

CASINO TAORO Parque de Taoro.
■ 2000-0300. ● 500 ptas.
Roulette, blackjack, other table games and slot machines, with restaurant and bar. Smart dress. Passport or ID card obligatory. Minimum age 18.

EL COLUMBUS Avenida de Colón 2.
■ 1800-0200.
Piano bar downstairs and a disco upstairs, attracting a select clientele.

EL COTO Hotel Botánico, Avenida Richard J. Yeoward.
■ 2200-0430 Sun.-Thu., 2200-0630 Fri. & Sat. ● 800-1000 ptas.
Jazz, salsa and disco music attracts a young, fashionable crowd to this stylish club with elegant tropical décor.

VICTORIA NIGHTCLUB Bajos Hotel, Avenida de Colón.
■ 2200-0430. ● Disco 800-1000 ptas.
Piano bar with terrace looking out over the sea. There's a disco in the basement playing slow music for a mature clientele.

COCO LOCO Hotel Maritim, El Burgado, Los Realejos.
■ 2000-0400. ● 800-1000 ptas.
Elegant disco, and bands playing requests. Popular with older age group.

CARRUSEL Edfo Valle Luz, Avenida de Melchor Luz.
■ 2200-0400. ● 800-1000 ptas.
The latest in modern international music, with a young, lively clientele.

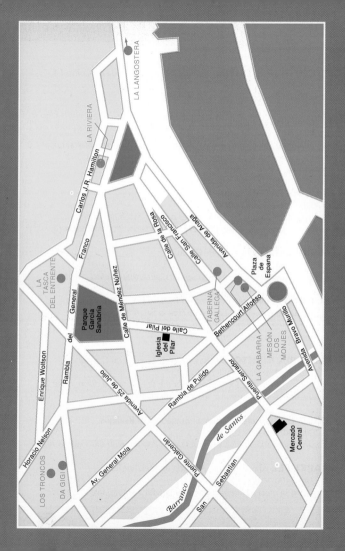

Santa Cruz

LA RIVIERA Rambla del General Franco 155.
■ 1200-1500, 2000-2400 Mon.-Sat. ● Expensive.
Top-quality French cuisine. Excellent service in elegant surroundings.

TABERNA GALLEGA c/ San Francisco 38.
■ 1300-1600, 2000-2400 Mon.-Sat. ● Moderate-Expensive.
Small family establishment serving fish of your own choice from northern Spain. Fishing boat décor.

LA GABARRA c/ Emilio Calzadilla 3.
■ 1200-1600, 2000-2400 Mon.-Sat. ● Moderate.
Surprisingly plain décor but excellent seafood dishes in this establishment which is patronized by the Santa Cruz elite.

MESÓN LOS MONJES c/ Marina 7.
■ 1200-1600, 2000-2400. ● Moderate.
Meat and fish dishes in Basque style, including a fine cod in squid sauce.

LOS TRONCOS c/ General Goded 17.
■ 1200-1600, 2000-2330. ● Inexpensive-Moderate.
The best place in town to sample typical Canarian cuisine. Specialities of the house include fish soup, cress soup and meat dishes.

LA LANGOSTERA San Andrés. 8 km northeast of Santa Cruz.
■ 1200-2300. Bus, taxi from c/ Marina. ● Inexpensive-Moderate.
You'll receive a warm welcome in this family-run fish restaurant offering excellent value, with specialities such as salted sea bream.

DA GIGI Rambla del General Franco 27.
■ 1200-1600, 1900-2400. ● Inexpensive.
Tasty home-made pizzas, with rapid but pleasant service.

LA TASCA DEL ENTRENTE c/ Dr Naveiras.
■ 1300-1600, 1900-0100. ● Inexpensive.
A tiny tapería offering snacks to the local business people. Try the chips mixed with beef, tortilla, tomato and garlic salad, and the local wine.

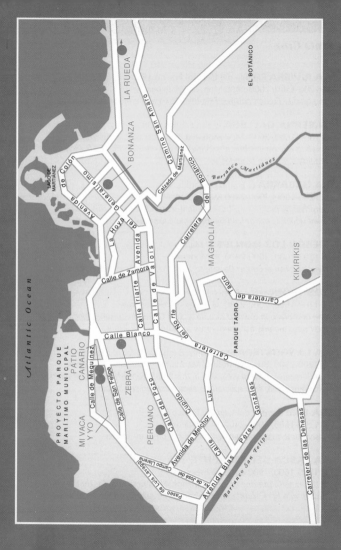

Puerto de la Cruz

MI VACA Y YO Cruz Verde 3.
■ 1830-2400. ● Expensive.
Tropical setting in which to enjoy excellent international cuisine which is worth the high prices. Try the lobster and wines.

MAGNOLIA Ctra del Botánico 5.
■ 1900-2400. ● Expensive.
Cordon bleu status – one of the best restaurants in town. Excellent Catalan and international dishes.

ZEBRA c/ Blanco 12-14.
■ 1200-1600, 1900-2300. ● Moderate.
Famous for its American-style pizzas. Good international cuisine.

LA RUEDA Ctra General del Norte, Sauzal.
■ 1200-1600, 1900-2400 Thu.-Tue. ● Moderate.
A family establishment where you can enjoy specialities of fresh barbecued meat and local mushrooms in a pleasant rustic atmosphere.

KIKIRIKIS Ctra Las Arenas.
■ 1900-0300 Mon.-Sat. ● Moderate.
Typical Canarian cuisine, including rabbit, chicken, etc.

PATIO CANARIO Cruz Verde 4.
■ 1300-2400 Wed.-Mon. ● Inexpensive-Moderate.
This restaurant serves a wide variety of both regional and international cuisine, including delicious fish brochettes. Cheerful, typically Canarian décor.

PERUANO Apertados San Miguel, c/ del Pozo.
■ 1200-1600, 1830-2300. ● Inexpensive-Moderate.
Fine Peruvian cuisine and a favourite with the locals.

BONANZA Edfo Avenida, Avenida del Generalísimo.
■ 1130-1600, 1800-2400. ● Inexpensive.
English steakhouse with a good choice and impeccable service.

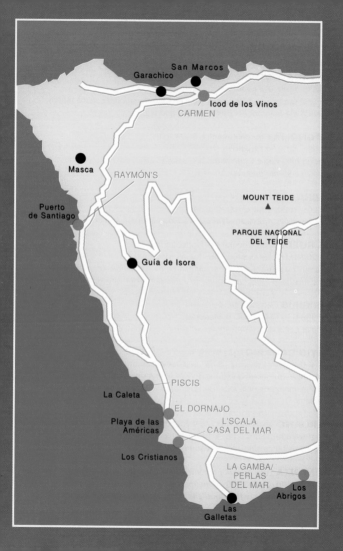

San Marcos

Garachico

Icod de los Vinos

CARMEN

Masca

RAYMÓN'S

MOUNT TEIDE ▲

Puerto
de Santiago

PARQUE NACIONAL
DEL TEIDE

Guía de Isora

PISCIS

La Caleta

EL DORNAJO

Playa de las
Américas

L'SCALA
CASA DEL MAR

Los Cristianos

LA GAMBA/
PERLAS
DEL MAR

Los
Abrigos

Las
Galletas

South & West

PISCIS La Caleta, near Adeje.
■ 1200-1700, 1900-2330. ● Moderate.
Delicious seafood, lobster and fresh fish, depending on the day's catch.
Live music and a Canarian show at night.

L'SCALA c/ La Paloma 7, Los Cristianos.
■ 1200-1530, 1800-2300. ● Moderate.
Stone-built restaurant whose specialities include steaks and suckling pig.

CASA DEL MAR Los Cristianos.
■ 1200-2300 Tue.-Sun. ● Moderate.
Distinctively-shaped restaurant with good views, serving fresh seafood.

LA GAMBA c/ La Marina, Los Abrigos.
■ 1200-2300 Tue.-Sun. ● Moderate.
Good location with a terrace overlooking the port of Los Abrigos.
Simple, but excellent value. Try the paella or seafood soup.

PERLAS DEL MAR c/ La Marina, Los Abrigos.
■ 1100-2300. ● Inexpensive-Moderate.
Another popular terrace restaurant where you can select your own fish.

EL DORNAJO Avenida Litoral, Playa de las Américas.
■ 1300-1600, 1900-2300. ● Inexpensive-Moderate.
The owner is also the chef of this successful Canarian-style restaurant.
Good reputation for its grilled meat and selection of fish and seafood.

CARMEN c/ Hércules 2, Icod de los Vinos.
■ 1200-2300 Thu.-Tue. ● Inexpensive.
In a beautiful Canarian house, restaurant offering various regional tapas
*(see **Food**) and dishes at extremely reasonable prices. See **EXCURSION 1**.*

RAYMÓN'S Avenida Marítima, Puerto de Santiago.
■ 1200-1600, 1930-2300. ● Inexpensive.
Terrace restaurant with attractive blue and white décor, and offering a
warm welcome. The salad, steaks and rosé wine are recommended.

RESTAURANTS 4

North

EL CAMPO Ctra General del Norte 342, Tacoronte.
▦ 1200-2400 Mon.-Sat., 1200-1500 Sun. ● Moderate.
A charming family establishment specializing in grilled meats.

LAS PALMERAS Camino Real 252, Agua García.
▦ 1200-1600, 1930-2300. ● Inexpensive-Moderate.
*Grills, fish served on wooden platters, and a variety of tapas (see **Food**).*

MI TASCA Camino Real 108, Agua García.
▦ 1100-2400/0100. ● Inexpensive-Moderate.
Good standard of food, and unusual specialities such as tripe.

LOLO El Prix, Tacoronte.
▦ 1200-1600, 2000-2400 Tue.-Sun. ● Inexpensive-Moderate.
*Canarian specialities, including baked potatoes, mojo picón and mojo verde (see **Food**). Friendly service and modern décor.*

LA HOYA DEL CAMELLO Ctra General 118, La Laguna.
▦ 1300-1600, 1900-2300 Tue.-Sun. ● Inexpensive-Moderate.
International and Spanish cuisine, both meat and fish. Friendly service.

EL JUNQUITO Ctra de Agua García 209, Tacoronte.
▦ 1200-2300. Closed Wed. & Sun. evening. ● Inexpensive.
Friendly atmosphere in this rustic restaurant serving grilled dishes.

CASA TOMÁS Camino del Portezuelo, La Laguna.
▦ 1200-2315 Tue.-Sun. ● Inexpensive.
Excellent value typical Canarian home-cooking.

DON POLLO El Calverio 73, La Esperanza.
▦ 1200-1600, 1900-2300. ● Inexpensive.
Almost entirely barbecued chicken dishes. Cosy, rustic atmosphere.

EL MECHAS Playa de Taganana. 21 km north of Santa Cruz.
▦ 1100-2300. Bus from c/ Marina, Santa Cruz. ● Inexpensive.
A tiny terraced restaurant on the beach. Simple and unpretentious.

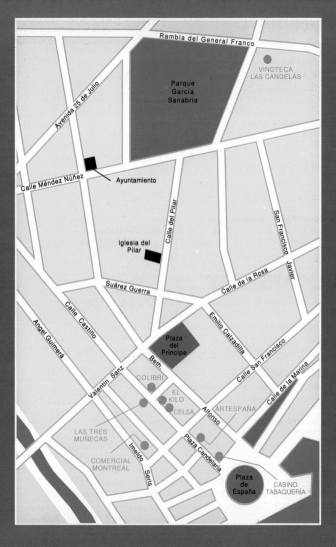

ARTESPAÑA Plaza de la Candelaria 8.
■ 0900-1300, 1600-1930 Mon.-Fri., 0900-1300 Sat.
State-subsidised craft shop selling a range of inexpensive local pottery, wood carvings, jewellery and paintings.

LAS TRES MUÑECAS c/ Castillo 15.
■ 0930-1300, 1600-2000 Mon.-Fri., 0930-1300 Sat.
*Large and crowded material shop selling silks and haberdashery. Of special interest at carnival time in Feb. and Mar. (see **Events**).*

EL KILO c/ Castillo 10.
■ 0900-1300, 1600-2000 Mon.-Fri., 0900-1300 Sat.
Another material shop. Has good range of seconds in sheets and towels.

COMERCIAL MONTREAL c/ Dr Allart 27.
■ 0930-1300, 1630-2000.
Good for Chinese silks and bargains in nightdresses, blouses, kimonos.

VINOTECA LAS CANDELAS Rambla del General Franco 114.
■ 0930-1300, 1700-2000 Mon.-Fri., 0930-1300 Sat.
Tastefully arranged wine shop with a wide selection from all over the world, as well as Spanish and local wines. Friendly and helpful staff.

COLIBRI c/ Castillo 20 & c/ Bethencourt Alfonso 6.
■ 0930-1300, 1630-2000 Mon.-Fri., 0930-1300 Sat.
Silk, wool, and leather clothing and accessories designed in-house. Much of it is exported to Paris and Madrid by the German proprietress.

CASINO TABAQUERÍA c/ de la Marina 1.
■ 0930-2000 Mon.-Fri., 0930-1300 Sat.
Fine tobacconists which also sells liqueurs, souvenirs and postcards.

CELSA c/ Castillo 8.
■ 0915-1300, 1600-1830 Mon.-Fri., 0915-1300 Sat.
Particularly good range of embroidery in Canarian and oriental styles. Some craftwork, ceramics and precious stones on sale in the basement.

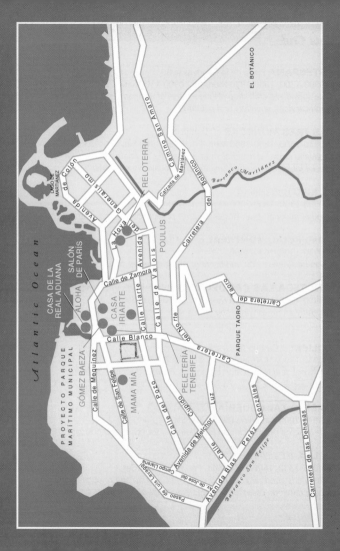

SALÓN DE PARIS c/ Quintana 13.
■ 0900-1300, 1600-2000 Mon.-Fri., 0900-1300 Sat.
Exotic collection of classic furs, with garments from all over the world.

PELETERIA TENERIFE c/ Quintana 3.
■ 0900-1300, 1700-2000 Mon.-Fri., 0900-1300 Sat.
Locally manufactured furs and leathers made to measure or off the peg.

CASA DE LA REAL ADUANA c/ Las Lonjas 1.
■ 0930-1300, 1600-1900 Mon.-Fri., 0930-1300 Sat.
Gifts of embroidery, gold and silverware. See ATTRACTIONS 3, WALK 3.

CASA IRIARTE c/ San Juan 21.
■ 0900-1300, 1600-1900 Mon.-Fri., 0900-1300 Sat.
Crafts centre with huge variety of goods. See ATTRACTIONS 3, WALK 3.

RELOTERRA Avenida del Generalisimo 16.
■ 1000-1300, 1600-2000 Mon.-Fri., 1000-1300 Sat.
Jewellery fashioned locally from imported stones.

POULUS c/ Enrique Talg 2.
■ 1000-1300, 1600-2000 Mon.-Fri., 1000-1300 Sat.
Jewellery from classical and expensive to affordable local designs.

GÓMEZ BAEZA c/ San Juan 10.
■ 0900-1300, 1600-2000 Mon.-Fri., 0900-1300 Sat.
The biggest department store in town, with household goods, clothes and furnishings displayed on six floors.

ALOHA c/ Santo Domingo 12.
■ 0900-1300, 1600-2000 Mon.-Fri., 0900-1300 Sat.
Beachwear and sports equipment, including surfboards.

MAMA MÍA c/ San Felipe 13.
■ 0900-1300, 1630-2000 Mon.-Fri., 0900-1300 Sat.
Local and international toys, with a selection of pushchairs for hire.

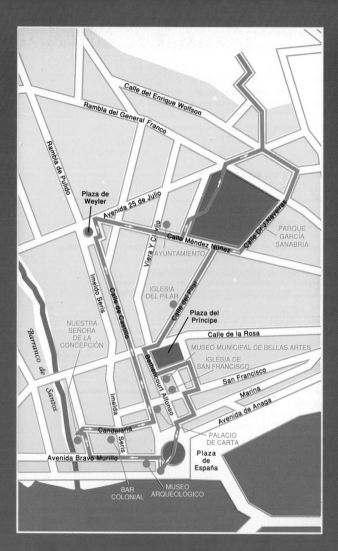

Santa Cruz

Duration: 2-3 hr.

Start from the small tourist office by the side of the Palacio Insular on Plaza de España. Notice the tall obelisk in front of you, the Monumento de los Caídos, in memoriam to those killed in the Spanish Civil War. The view from the top is splendid but unfortunately the monument is rarely open. On the left is the main entrance to the Palacio Insular, the Canary Islands' administrative offices, where you can see a model of Tenerife. Turn left down the side of the building into Avenida Bravo Murillo and the first door on your left is the entrance to the Museo Arqueológico (see **ATTRACTIONS 1**). Continue along the avenue and to the right you'll see the modest whitewashed exterior of Nuestra Señora de la Concepción (see **ATTRACTIONS 1, A-Z**), with its sedate and imposing bell tower. The entrance to the church is on c/ del Puente del Cabo. On Plaza de la Iglesia is what remains of the original city buildings (presently undergoing renovation), which are quite charming with their wooden balconies in the colonial style. Outside the church, turn right and head along c/ Candelaria. Just before you cross c/ Imelda Seris, you will see the Bar Colonial tucked away on a corner to your right. It's worth stopping to admire its interesting curios. Further along you'll pass the large department store, Maya, before going straight on to Plaza de la Candelaria. Of architectural interest is the renovated building, now used by the Banco Español de Crédito, known as the Palacio de Carta (see **ATTRACTIONS 1, A-Z**). Walk up the pedestrian precinct of c/ del Castillo at the top of the square, and browse through its many shops (see **SHOPPING 1**). At the far end is Plaza de Weyler with its pretty marble fountain and overlooked by the impressive building of the Canary Islands military HQ. Turn first right at the far end of the square along c/ Méndez Núñez. This contains the civil government buildings on your left and the handsome façade of the Ayuntamiento (Town Hall) next to it on the corner. Continue towards the Parque García Sanabria (see **ATTRACTIONS 1**) where you can relax in the leafy shade of the tropical plants and have a refreshing cool drink. For the energetic there is a pleasant walk up Avenida 25 de Julio on the opposite side of Rambla del General Franco to the north of the park. Bear left up the narrow, steep c/ Fernando Barajas Vilches and climb out of town through the desirable residential area. A 20-30 min walk will reward you with a splendid view over the city and port. On the way back down, turn sharp left into c/ del Enrique Wolfson to admire the beautiful colonial-style town houses and their pastel colours. Turn right into c/ Dr J. Naveiras, which will return you to the front entrance of the park. Head along c/ del Pilar and admire the chic clothes and shoe boutiques. On your right, with its undistinguished façade but interesting interior, is the Iglesia del Pilar (see **ATTRACTIONS 1**). c/ del Pilar takes you past the large Galerías Preciados store and leads on to the side of Plaza del Príncipe. On the opposite side of the square is the Museo Municipal de Bellas Artes (see **ATTRACTIONS 1**) in c/ José Murphy. To the back of the museum is the Iglesia de San Francisco (see **ATTRACTIONS 1**), on the square of the same name. Turn left along c/ Hervas and c/ Villalba and you will return to Plaza de España.

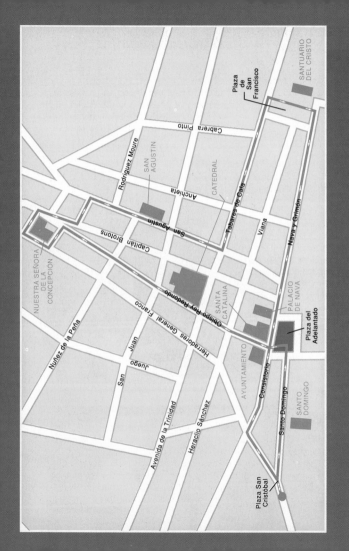

La Laguna

Duration: 2-3 hr.

Starting from the terminus of the Santa Cruz bus on Calvo Sotelo, cross over Plaza San Cristóbal and make the gentle ascent of c/ Santo Domingo. On your right is the monastery of Santo Domingo (see **ATTRACTIONS 2**), notable for its Plateresque style of architecture and ancient dragon tree (see

Drago) in the gardens.
Continue up the street to
Plaza del Adelantado, an
exceptionally beautiful
square bordered by build-
ings of historical interest.
The most striking of these
is the registry office, with
its magnificent carved
wooden balcony, so typi-
cal of the architecture of
the Canary Islands. Next
to it stands the market,
and diagonally across the
shady square stands the
17thC façade of the
Palacio de Nava, of pure
Baroque style and stately
elegance. Next to it is the
16th-17thC monastery of
Santa Catalina, and to the
left of the monastery on
the opposite side of the

road is the recently restored Ayuntamiento (see **ATTRACTIONS 2**). The entrance is on c/ Obispo Rey Redondo, which leads off the square, and the interior contains frescoes which depict the history of the island. Continue along c/ Obispo Rey Redondo, known by the locals as La Carrera (The Street), and glance down its side streets at some of the handsome buildings for which La Laguna is justly renowned. The third turning on the right opens out into Plaza Fray Albino, on which stands

the Catedral (see **ATTRACTIONS 2**, **A-Z**). The setting in the square is tran-
quillity itself, as the townsfolk relax on benches and watch the world
go by. The neoclassical façade is by Ventura Rodríguez, and dates from
the early 20thC. The twin bell towers are a landmark. Continue along
c/ Obispo Rey Redondo towards the six-tiered square brick tower of
Nuestra Señora de la Concepción (see **ATTRACTIONS 2**, **A-Z**), visible at
the end of the street. The main entrance is on the left, on Plaza Dr
Oliviera. This is La Laguna's oldest church, and surely its most beautiful. Return to the front of the church on Plaza de la Concepción and
take the left-hand fork along c/ Capitán Brotons. Turn first left down
Ascanio y Nieves into c/ San Agustín. On the left is the solemn façade
of the 17thC church of San Agustín (see **ATTRACTIONS 2**), all that
remains after a fire at the beginning of this century. Visit the beautiful
cloister of the former monastery, which is to the left of the church. Back
outside, turn left and then take the second turning on the left,
c/ Tabares de Cala, which leads on to the impressive open square of
Plaza de San Francisco. Diagonally opposite and a little set back from
the square is the Santuario del Cristo (see **ATTRACTIONS 2**), housing the
15thC statue of Santísimo Cristo de la Laguna (see **A-Z**). To return to the
bus terminus, take c/ Nava y Grimón, which leads to Plaza del
Adelantado, and continue along c/ Consistorio back to Plaza San
Cristóbal.

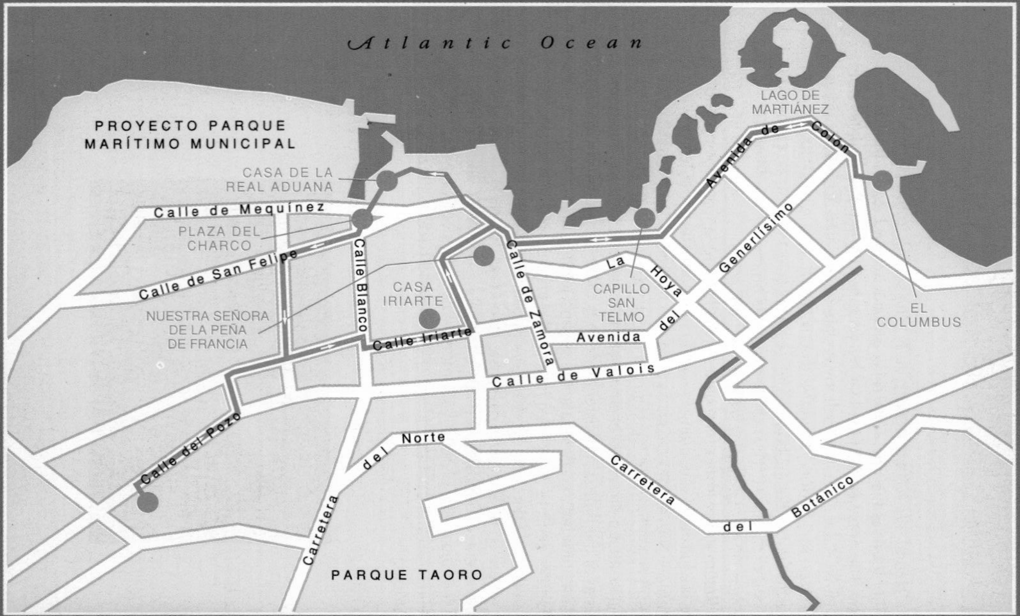

Atlantic Ocean

PROYECTO PARQUE MARÍTIMO MUNICIPAL

LAGO DE MARTIANEZ

EL COLUMBUS

Avenida de Colón

Genetísimo

La Hoya

CAPILLO SAN TELMO

Avenida del

Calle de Valois

Calle de Zamora

CASA IRIARTE

Calle Iriarte

Calle Blanco

CASA DE LA REAL ADUANA

Calle de Mequinez

PLAZA DEL CHARCO

Calle de San Fel...pe

NUESTRA SEÑORA DE LA PEÑA DE FRANCIA

Calle del Pozo

Carretera del Botánico

PARQUE TAORO

Carretera del Norte

Puerto de la Cruz

Duration: 2-3 hr.

From the bus station on c/ del Pozo, take c/ Dr Ingram, a street of many shops and restaurants, which leads into c/ Iriarte. This has fine examples of 18thC Canarian architecture, among the best of which is the Palacio Ventosa, set in a small square on the right. It is an elegant stone and wood structure which now houses a seminary. Opposite is Casa Iriarte (see **ATTRACTIONS 3**, **SHOPPING 2**), the birthplace of the author Tomás de Iriarte (1750-91), which now contains many craft shops. Continue up the picturesque flight of steps on c/ Iriarte and turn left into c/ Cologan, leading to Plaza de la Peña de Francia. The square is bordered by the post office and tourist office. The bust in the centre is of Agustín de Bethencourt y Molina (1758-1824), a locally born inventor and engineer. Once inside Nuestra Señora de la Peña de Francia (see **ATTRACTIONS 3**), which backs onto the square, you'll see some beautiful wooden figurines and a fine Baroque altarpiece. From the church, turn right and take c/ de San Telmo along the seafront. You soon come to the Capilla San Telmo, a fishermen's chapel built in 1626. On the left is the Lago de Martiánez complex (see **CHILDREN**). If you wish, continue along Avenida de Colón until you reach El Columbus on the left (see **NIGHTLIFE**). Here you could sample some of the delicious pastries while enjoying an unimpeded view of the sea. Alternatively, retrace your steps through the craft and souvenir stalls of c/ de San Telmo. At the end of the promenade a popular pastime is to watch the waves break spectacularly against the rocks on Playa de San Telmo (see **BEACHES 2**). From here, bear right down c/ de Santo Domingo to enter the older part of town. At the bottom, turn right onto c/ Las Lonjas. At the foot of this picturesque cobbled street is Casa de la Real Aduana (see **ATTRACTIONS 3**, **SHOPPING 2**). The charming fishing port, Puerto Pesquero, is a small stretch of sand protected by two breakwaters and harbouring small fishing boats which add a touch of colour to the scene. Once it served as a port for La Orotava and handled 80% of the island's trade. Bear left towards Plaza del Charco (see **ATTRACTIONS 3**), bordered by 18thC buildings. From here, you can wander through the charming streets of the old town, with its boutiques and restaurants, before bearing west to return to the bus station.

Mount Teide

Duration: 3-4 hr.

The ascent of Mount Teide (see **EXCURSION 2**, **A-Z**) via Montaña Blanca is strenuous in places, so bring proper climbing boots, warm clothing and a supply of water. The road doesn't end until deceptively high up into the mountains, so it is easy to forget that you are climbing at altitudes of 2300-3700 m. The cable car will not operate on windy days, so check the weather prospects before setting out. For information, consult the Centro de Visitantes at El Portillo.

Take Bus 348 (0830 Wed.-Sun. from Puerto de la Cruz) and alight at the Montaña Blanca stop. A notice board gives an outline of the network of paths. The ascent begins with a pleasant climb along a gravel path with views back to Las Cañadas (see **A-Z**) and of the mountains to the north and cliffs on the northeast coast. After 60-70 min turn right at the signpost for the Refugio de Altavista. The path becomes rougher and the ascent steeper as it traverses the terrain above the floor of the crater of Las Cañadas. After 60 min or so of hard climbing over pitted, sandy-coloured stone and pebbles, you will reach the mountain refuge (accommodation bookings from tourist office). Continue along the path behind the refuge through a landscape littered with large boulders. On the right after 10-15 min is a path leading to the Cueva del Hielo, with its ice stalactites. Back on the original path, the slope levels out and you come to a fork where you should continue straight on. Shortly afterwards you'll see the cable car terminus below on the left. Turn right when you get to the main path up to the summit. Cracks in the ground emit steam and the air is filled with the odour of sulphur. You arrive at the summit, which consists of a small crater, after 45-60 min. To the southwest is Pico Viejo, in gentle hues of mauve and brown, and below is the floor of Las Cañadas crater, revealing the stark beauty of its barren landscape. At 3717 m, you're above the clouds and flight paths. On a clear day the view embraces Gomera, La Palma, Hierro and Gran Canaria (see **ISLANDS**, **A-Z**). When you've had enough of the majestic views and buffeting of the wind, make the 20 min descent towards the cable car terminus (last descent 1600). Here you can have a drink while you wait your turn. The descent takes 8 min and you can then catch Bus 348 back to Puerto de la Cruz.

FABRICA D

PLAYA DE

GON

Anaga Mountains: A mountain range in the northeastern corner of Tenerife, peaking at over 1000 m. The steep slopes and deep gullies are spectacular, and the lower hillsides lush with vegetation, as in the Las Mercedes forest. Of the numerous viewpoints, Pico del Inglés is perhaps the best. The mountains offer many good walks for the active holiday-maker and buses to the region leave Santa Cruz from Avenida de Anaga by Plaza de España. See **EXCURSION 3**.

Bajamar: 30 km northeast of Puerto de la Cruz. One of the more out-of-the-way tourist resorts to the northeast of the island, set on cliffs beneath the impressive backdrop of the Anaga mountains (see **A-Z**), and with modern apartments and hotels spreading towards the nearby Punta del Hidalgo. A quiet spot of fishing is a popular pastime on the seafront, where there is also a tiny beach in a protected cove, and sea-water swimming pools. See **EXCURSION 3**.

Banana Plantations: The banana has been vital to the economy of the Canary Islands for more than a hundred years, having been intro-duced from Indochina in the latter part of the 19thC. Recently, produc-tion and marketing difficulties have necessitated government interven-tion in the form of subsidies. The industry still appears to be in danger and many farmers are turning to other crops. Most of the remaining banana plantations are in the north (see **EXCURSION 3**) and on La Palma (see **EXCURSION 4**). The tour of Bananera El Guanche (see **CHILDREN**) gives an interesting insight into the process of banana cultivation.

Barranco del Infierno: An immense and beautiful gorge near the town of Adeje in the southwest of Tenerife. It provides a very popular walk which few people will find too strenuous. See **EXCURSION 1**.

Bethencourt, Jean de (1359-1425): A Norman nobleman, he set off in 1402 to conquer the Canary Islands, under the orders of King Henry III of Castile. Having captured Lanzarote (see **A-Z**), he was named 'King of the Canaries' by Henry, and went on to take Fuerteventura (see **A-Z**) and Hierro (see **A-Z**) in 1405. His attempt to conquer Gran Canaria (see **A-Z**) the following year failed, and the final conquest was left to Isabella and Ferdinand, in 1483.

Bobadilla, Beatriz de (15thC): A significant figure in the Canary Islands' history. She and her husband, Hernán Peraza the Younger, displayed great cruelty towards the islanders while governing Gomera (see **A-Z**). Beatriz was forced to retreat to the safety of the Torre del Conde in San Sebastián following an uprising in 1488, during which Hernán was killed. Following the re-establishment of her authority she entertained the explorer Columbus (see **A-Z**) during his visits to Gomera and speculation remains that they had an affair. Her powerful position was confirmed by her marriage to Alonso Fernández de Lugo (see **A-Z**) in 1498.

Buenavista: 35 km west of Puerto de la Cruz. An archetypal small Canarian community, nestling beneath the Teno mountain range. You can sample a real taste of village life here as children play in the tree-lined square beside the town's church, Virgen de los Remedios, which houses a fine painting of St. Francis. A track leads from the village to the westernmost tip of the island at Punta de Teno, going past the Mirador de Don Pompeyo which offers a scenic prospect back to the town. The road from Buenavista to Santiago del Teide is one of the most spectacular on the island as it rises through the Valle del Palmar. See **EXCURSION 1**.

Canarian Wrestling: *Lucha Canaria* is a sport originating in ancient Egyptian or Guanche (see **A-Z**) times. Two barefoot contestants face each other within a circle of 10 m diameter. The aim is to grasp one's adversary and throw him to the ground. Much ritual precedes the contest and the scoring system is sufficiently complicated to make it difficult for the uninitiated to predict the winner before the judge announces his decision. Demonstrations of Canarian wrestling are held regularly and are a popular feature of some fiestas.

Canary Islands: Situated in an area some 100-300 km off the northwest African coast, the seven main islands in the group are (from east to west) Lanzarote, Fuerteventura, Gran Canaria, Tenerife, Gomera, La Palma and Hierro. The ancient title of the archipelago was the Blessed or Fortunate Islands, but the true origin of the name Canary Islands is still uncertain. Suggestions are that the Romans gave the islands their title after the Latin for dog, *canis*, or that they were named after *canna*, an indigenous plant. Canary birds, or *canora*, were named after the islands. See the **ISLANDS** topic page and the **A-Z** entry for each island.

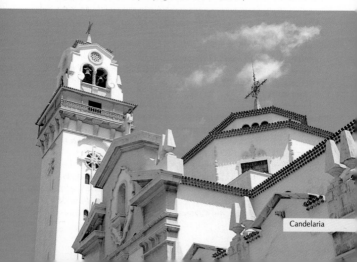

Candelaria

Candelaria: 20 km southwest of Santa Cruz. A small fishing town built on a hillside situated just beneath (but hidden from) the Autopista del Sur. In Aug., pilgrims from all over the Canaries converge on the Basílica de Nuestra Señora de la Candelaria (see **ATTRACTIONS 4**). It is set on an open square with a fountain and artificial waterfall to one side. The square is bordered by pleasant cafés and whitewashed houses with carved balconies. On the seafront, red stone statues of Guanche (see **A-Z**) kings stand with their backs to Candelaria's small pebbly beach. The basilica, a modern church, features frescoes, small rounded stained-glass windows, imposing stone arches, and a delightful small wooden carved and painted pulpit. The chief attraction, however, is the statue of Nuestra Señora de la Candelaria (see **A-Z**), glittering in the splendour of her pedestal.

Catedral, La Laguna: The cathedral was founded in the 16thC and rebuilt in the early 20thC with a neoclassical façade and well-proportioned pseudo-Gothic interior. It houses a fine statue of St. Christopher by Fernando Estévez (1788-1854) and a sculpted marble pulpit (1767). Other features include a splendid organ (London, 1857) and neoclassical choir stalls. The most striking work of art is the enormous Baroque altarpiece, La Virgen de los Remedios, flanked by Flemish paintings and set off by a richly-embossed silver altar. See **ATTRACTIONS 2, WALK 2**.

Columbus, Christopher (1451-1506): At the beginning of his expedition that led to the discovery of America in 1492, Columbus stopped at Las Palmas on Gran Canaria (see **A-Z**) for supplies and repairs. It was the first of four such visits he was to pay to the Canaries, giving rise to the rumour that he was in love with the Spanish exile, Beatriz de Bobadilla (see **A-Z**). The house in which he is said to have resided can be seen in San Sebastián on Gomera (see **EXCURSION 5**).

Cristo de los Dolores: Housed in the chapel of a former Augustinian monastery in Tacoronte (see **ATTRACTIONS 4, EXCURSION 3**), this 17thC statue was modelled on an engraving by the German artist, Albrecht Dürer (1471-1528). It was brought to the island from Madrid by Thomas Pereida in 1662 and depicts a resurrected Christ clasping the crucifix in his arms. It is a particularly beautiful and original image, and is much revered by the islanders.

Drago: The Spanish name for the dragon tree or *Dracaena draco*. On Tenerife there are several specimens of this strange-looking tree which often has a huge trunk, crowned with a thick mass of dagger-like leaves. A survivor from the Tertiary era, it is extremely difficult to grow elsewhere. The blood-red sap was used by the Guanches (see **A-Z**) in medicines and mummifying fluid. The most famous *drago* is at Icod de los Vinos (see **ATTRACTIONS 4**, **EXCURSION 1**), and there are other fine examples at La Laguna (see **ATTRACTIONS 2**, **WALK 2**) and Tacoronte (see **EXCURSION 3**).

Esperanza Forest: An impressive forest with a variety of trees, including pine and eucalyptus, and with a good road leading up along the central spine of the island from La Laguna to Las Cañadas. The several excellent viewpoints are ideal for picnics. See **EXCURSION 2**.

Fernández de Lugo, Alonso (1456-1525): A nobleman from Andalucía entrusted with the task of subjecting the Canary Islands to Spanish rule in the late 15thC. He founded the town of Las Palmas on Gran Canaria (see **A-Z**) in 1487, and went on to invade Tenerife on 1 May 1492, landing at what is now Santa Cruz. It took him four years to conquer the island and he established the town of La Laguna (see **A-Z**) as capital in 1496. He also introduced the parallel grid street system. He married Beatriz de Bobadilla (see **A-Z**) in 1498.

Fuerteventura: The nearest of all the Canary Islands to the coast of Africa, and possessing the longest coastline. With its wide stretches of sand and numerous beaches, it is a haven for those who enjoy swimming, scuba diving, windsurfing and fishing. There is little in the way of nightlife, so Fuerteventura is also ideal for those simply seeking peace and quiet. The island reaches its highest point of 800 m at the Peninsula de Jandía in the southwest. Places of interest include the dunes of Corralejo and the island's historical capital of Betancuria, named after Jean de Bethencourt (see **A-Z**). See **ISLANDS**.

Drago de Icod

Garachico: 26 km west of Puerto de la Cruz. Garachico, formerly an important port on the north coast, was largely destroyed by a volcanic eruption in 1706. It was rebuilt on a semicircular mass of lava protruding into the sea and has managed to retain much of its original charm. Older buildings include the 17thC palace of the Marquis of Adeje, and Iglesia de Santa Ana, which houses some important works by the Canarian sculptor, Luján Pérez (1756-1815). The 16thC Castillo de San Miguel (1000-1900), situated on the seafront, is also worth a visit and has embroidery and other souvenirs on sale. There are natural-rock swimming pools in the neighbourhood. See **EXCURSION 1**.

Gomera: The closest island to Tenerife and usually visible from the west coast. It has a rocky coastline and mountainous interior. Gomera is famous for *silbo*, the unique whistling language the locals use to communicate with each other from hilltop to hilltop, often over considerable distances. *Silbo* is sadly dying out as a living language but has been retained as a unique tourist attraction. The capital town of San Sebastián has a population of 7000. From here Christopher Columbus (see **A-Z**) set off on his journey to America in 1492, a fact commemorated by a national monument in the former fortress of Torre del Conde.

Gomera

The verdant Valle Hermigua to the east of the island and the terraced slopes of the Valle Gran Rey contain the most striking scenery on the island. The ferry to San Sebastián from Los Cristianos on Tenerife is often crowded with visitors but tourism has had only a limited effect on the islanders' peaceful way of life. However, an airport is scheduled for completion in the forseeable future. See **EXCURSION 5**, **ISLANDS**.

Gran Canaria: Situated between Tenerife and Fuerteventura, Gran Canaria is an island of stark contrasts, with mountains, arid plains, tropical vegetation, cliffs, ravines and fertile valleys. It is an increasingly popular and busy destination for holiday-makers. The capital, Las Palmas, offers museums, churches and an old quarter of typical Canarian buildings to wander through at your leisure, as well as a bustling social life of nightclubs and restaurants. There are also some fine beaches, notably at Maspalomas. See **ISLANDS**.

Guanches: When the first explorers arrived on the islands in the 13thC, the Guanches were comparable to a Stone-Age people, with only rudimentary tools and utensils, an apparent absence of written language (though some undeciphered symbols have been discovered), and natural cave dwellings formed in the lava flows. They kept goats, sheep, pigs and dogs, and their diet consisted mainly of *gofio* (see **Food**), meat and goat's cheese. Guanche society was patriarchal, with a king (*mencey*) at the head of the territorial units, of which there were eight on Tenerife at the time of the Spanish conquest in the 15thC. It is thought that they were sun and moon worshippers. Evidence of a convent of priestesses has been found on Gran Canaria (see **A-Z**). One of the most fascinating aspects of Guanche culture is the fact that they mummified their dead – a practice otherwise known only to the Egyptians and Peruvians. The bodies were left to dry in the sun, treated with herbs and ointments, and wrapped in skins. They were then left, with their possessions, in virtually inaccessible caves. This practice suggests that they held a belief in life after death. The Museo Arqueológico in Santa Cruz (see **ATTRACTIONS 1**) provides an interesting background to Guanche culture, with displays of artefacts and historical findings from the island.

Hierro: This tiny triangular island consists of a central plateau, culminating in the summit of Mount Mal Paso at 1320 m, and open coast to the north forming a 14 km bay, El Golfo. The charming county town of Valverde has a population of 5000, and its 18thC fortified church contains an admirable statue of the Virgin. In the 17thC the westernmost tip of Hierro, La Punta de Orchilla, was designated the original prime meridian (0 degrees longitude), as the island was considered to be the end of the world. It was from Hierro that Columbus (see **A-Z**) set sail for his second voyage of discovery to the New World in 1493. See **ISLANDS**.

Icod de los Vinos: 22 km west of Puerto de la Cruz. A pleasant town in the centre of an area noted for wine and banana production. It contains the most famous dragon tree or *drago* on the island (see **ATTRACTIONS 4, A-Z**), which is carefully tended and attracts many sightseers. Also of interest are the 15th-16thC Iglesia de San Marcos, with its Renaissance façade, and the adjacent Franciscan monastery. See **ATTRACTIONS 4, EXCURSION 1**.

Jardín Botánico, Puerto de la Cruz: One of the most comprehensive collections of tropical plants in the world, displayed in just 2.5 hectares of gardens at Carretera del Botánico. The Marquis Villaneuva de Prado founded the gardens in 1788 under the orders of King Charles III of Spain, and they flourished in the climate of the Canary Islands. An immense rubber tree, over 200 years old, stands on a tangle of roots. Orchids thrive in the greenhouse, there's a cactus corner, and birdsong adds to the atmosphere. See **ATTRACTIONS 3**.

La Laguna: 8 km west of Santa Cruz. A university and cathedral town, its full name is San Cristóbal de la Laguna, and it is Tenerife's second-largest town, after Santa Cruz. Founded in the late 15thC by the Spanish conqueror Alonso Fernández de Lugo (see **A-Z**), and the capital of the island until 1723, it is designed on a grid street system. La Laguna boasts some fine examples of colonial architecture and is famous for its Corpus Christi celebrations in May and June, when carpets of sand and petals are laid in the streets (see **Events**). It has

Jardín Botánico

retained much of its original character and exists independently of the tourism which characterizes many of the island's other towns and resorts. See **ATTRACTIONS 2, EXCURSION 3, WALK 2**.

Lanzarote: The most distinctly volcanic island of the archipelago, with its preponderance of lava fields splashed with the colour of the local vegetation. This grows in remarkable abundance thanks to an ingenious agricultural method which uses the thin layers of volcanic ash to create the necessary moisture for plants to grow. Lanzarote is largely flat and therefore there is a constant refreshing breeze blown in from the shores of Africa. The island's attractions include camel rides up into the volcanic range of Montañas de Fuego (Fire Mountains), coastal caves and lagoons, and some excellent beaches. See **ISLANDS**.

La Orotava: 8 km south of Puerto de la Cruz. One of the oldest towns on the island, nestling among the banana plantations (see A-Z) of the valley, and now a major crafts centre. Casa de los Balcones has superbly-carved wooden balconies and a display of embroidery work in its patio. It was in La Orotava that the tradition started of creating unique works of art from flowers and sand for the Corpus Christi celebrations (see **Events**). The parish church of Nuestra Señora de la Concepción (see **A-Z**) has an impressive façade and contains many treasures, and the Hospital de la Santísima Trinidad offers a splendid view of the valley below. See **ATTRACTIONS 4, EXCURSION 1**.

La Palma: Compared to other islands of its size, La Palma boasts some of the world's highest peaks and one of the largest known volcanic craters, La Caldera de Taburiente (770 m deep and 28 km in circumference), now a national park and covered in pine woods. The capital, Santa Cruz de La Palma, has a population of 15,000 and is located on the eastern coast. The picturesque houses and magnificent examples of 16thC architecture, as seen in the town hall and church of San Salvador, make it a charming town to visit. La Palma's economy is based on bananas, tobacco and cigars, and its activities as a port. Tourism is also quietly expanding. See **EXCURSION 4, ISLANDS**.

Las Cañadas: An old volcanic crater formed millions of years ago and made into a national park in 1954. The exterior ridge is made up of steep craggy walls, and encloses a chaotic and arid plateau of strange rock formations and gravel plains 2215 m above sea level. It measures 16 km across and 45 km round the perimeter. The most recent volcanic activity was at the end of the 18thC. The Centro de Visitantes near El Portillo to the northeast of the crater (0900-1600) provides film shows, photos, samples, explanations of how the crater is thought to have been formed, and guided walks by arrangement. For further information, contact the information service at La Laguna, tel: 259903/263898. See **EXCURSION 2, Parque Nacional del Teide**.

Las Raíces: An obelisk in a clearing of Esperanza forest (see **A-Z**) which marks the spot where an event took place that was to dramatically affect the history of Spain. Here, in June 1936, Gen. Franco held a meeting of military leaders to determine their loyalty in supporting him against the government. See **EXCURSION 2**.

Los Cristianos

Los Cristianos: 75 km southwest of Santa Cruz. A new and bustling resort built around an old port, and now merging along the coastline with neighbouring Playa de las Américas (see **A-Z**). There are numerous shops and inexpensive restaurants. The beach is well maintained and offers all forms of water sports. Its shallow waters are ideal for children (see **BEACHES 1**). From the port it is possible to take the ferry to the island of Gomera (see **EXCURSION 5, A-Z**).

Los Gigantes: 55 km west of Puerto de la Cruz. A pleasant town on the west coast, set beneath the impressive cliffs of the same name. It has an air of prosperity and consists mainly of private villas and timeshare apartments. There is a yachting marina lined with restaurants, shops and cafés, and a small beach of black sand where pedalos are available for hire. Both Los Gigantes and nearby Puerto de Santiago offer the chance of quiet and relaxing holidays. See **EXCURSION 1**.

Los Realejos: 6 km west of Puerto de la Cruz. A town comprised of two settlements, Realejo Alto and Realejo Bajo, originally the camps of the opposing armies of the Guanches (see **A-Z**) and the Spanish conquistadores, and the site of Tenerife's last battle in 1496. Los Realejos contains one of the oldest churches on the island, Iglesia de Santiago, built by order of the conquering Andalusian nobleman Alonso Fernández de Lugo (see **A-Z**). The church houses three painted panels thought to be by the Anvers School (16thC). See **EXCURSION 1**.

Mount Teide: Pronounced to rhyme with 'lady'. At 3717 m, this is the highest mountain in Spain, with a volcanic crater last active at the end of the 18thC. Mount Teide was formed after a number of eruptions, by Chahorra in particular, and rose out of the crater, La Rambleta. During the winter months the peak is often snowcapped, providing an unusual background to the sunbaked plains of the south. It is possible to walk up to the edge of the crater (50 m in diameter, 25 m deep) from the terminus of the cable car at 3555 m. Queues for the cable car can be lengthy, so it may be best either to make an early start and arrive before the first run at 0900 or wait until mid-afternoon when the queues have often shortened. The last cable car is at 1600. Strong winds can prevent it from operating, so check the weather before departing. The cable car also carries a warning against use by those suffering from heart disease. See **EXCURSION 2**, **WALK 4**, **Parque Nacional del Teide**.

Natural History: The flora of the Canary Islands varies according to the altitude and the localized climate. More than 30% of the species are unique to the islands, and authentic survivors from the Tertiary era can be found, for example *laurelsilva* or laurelwood, which is impossible to find outside the archipelago. In the arid, low-lying regions of Tenerife (particularly the south), the vegetation includes cacti and palm trees. Dragon trees (see **Drago**) also grow at fairly low altitudes. In the centre and north the flora is distributed in ascending layers, with laurelwood giving way to bog myrtle and briar. Above 1000 m pines appear, including the *pinus Canariensis*, a fire-resistant species which provides much of the wood used in the manufacture of the carved balconies to be seen all over the island. Agriculture is still one of the main sources of income, and banana plantations (see **A-Z**), vineyards and tobacco fields are to be seen in the valley regions. Flowers are grown in abundance in the lusher parts of the island, adding wonderful splashes of colour. The most spectacular of these is the *strelitzia* or bird of paradise flower, which can be packaged for you to take home at a very reasonable cost.

Nelson, Horatio (1758-1805): The famous British admiral sailed into Santa Cruz on Tenerife in 1797 in an attempt to capture a Spanish treasure ship said to be lying in the harbour. Two hundred and twenty-six sailors died in the unsuccessful assault, and Nelson lost part of his arm and was forced to retreat. The flags of his ships are preserved in Nuestra Señora de la Concepción in Santa Cruz (see **ATTRACTIONS 1**, **WALK 1**, **A-Z**), and the famous cannon, El Tigre (reputed to be the one which injured Nelson), can be seen at the military museum, Castillo de Paso Alto, in Santa Cruz (see **ATTRACTIONS 1**).

Nuestra Señora de la Candelaria: According to legend, a statue of the Virgin was washed up on the shore at Candelaria (see **A-Z**) in the 14thC and became an object of worship for the Guanches (see **A-Z**), who were unaware of its Christian significance. It was housed in a cave (today known as San Blas) and later in a sanctuary near the present church, where it was venerated until 1826 when it was carried out to sea by a tidal wave. The statue seen today, and housed in the sumptuous Basílica de Nuestra Señora de la Candelaria (see **ATTRACTIONS 4**), is a copy carved by Fernando Estévez soon after the loss of the original. It attracts many pilgrims from all over the Canary Islands every Aug. (see **Events**).

Nuestra Señora de la Concepción, La Laguna: This early-16thC church is one of the most beautiful on the island. Crowned by a six-tiered tower, it is built in typical Canarian style with three naves, and features a magnificent *Mudéjar* wood ceiling and a 17thC sculpted Baroque pulpit. Among its many treasures are several statues by Fernando Estévez (1788-1854) and some unique 15thC varnished ceramic baptismal fonts. See **ATTRACTIONS 2**, **EXCURSION 3**.

Nuestra Señora de la Concepción, La Orotava: Behind the twin-towered Baroque façade of this 18thC church stands a remarkable high altar fashioned out of marble and alabaster by the Italian sculptor, Giuseppe Gagini. Other works of art are the 17thC Baroque altarpiece of the Virgin sculpted in wood by Lázaro Gonzales, and several examples of 18th and 19thC Canarian sculpture, including work by Luján Pérez (1756-1815). See **ATTRACTIONS 4**, **EXCURSION 1**.

Playa de las Américas

Nuestra Señora de la Concepción, Santa Cruz: Originally built in the 16thC, the church was destroyed by fire in the 17thC and required extensive renovation. Today's building is largely of the 18thC and consists of a low nave with four aisles. The marble pulpit encrusted with jasper is particularly fine, as is the richly-worked high altar with a sculpture by Luján Pérez (1756-1815) depicting the Virgin Mary grieving for Christ. There are also several paintings dating from the 17th to the 19thC. Among other treasures are the flags captured from Nelson (see **A-Z**) after his defeat in 1797, and relics of the conquest of Tenerife by Alonso Fernández de Lugo (see **A-Z**). See **ATTRACTIONS 1, WALK 1**.

Palacio de Carta: Originally built in 1742 by Don Matías Bernardo Carta, general treasurer of the Real Ciudad, the building was bought and restored by the Banco Español de Crédito and constitutes one of the finest typically Canarian buildings in Santa Cruz. See **ATTRACTIONS 1, WALK 1**.

Parque Nacional del Teide: Consisting of the Las Cañadas crater (see **A-Z**) and Mount Teide itself (see **WALK 4, A-Z**), the park contains an almost supernatural or lunar landscape which has been used as the location for science fiction films. The area was established as a national park in 1954. Apart from the simple splendour of its scenery, it is also of great geological and botanical interest. The Centro de Visitantes near El Portillo (see **EXCURSION 2**) offers a permanent exhibition covering the history of the area, and produces information leaflets concerning the park's network of walks and footpaths. Guided tours can also be arranged. As a national park, it has various restrictions in force on, for instance, the collection of rock and plant specimens, the lighting of fires, and camping. The visitor centre also advises against tourists undertaking walks and climbs without proper clothing, equipment and supplies.

Playa de las Américas: 75 km southwest of Santa Cruz. A purpose-built resort on the southwest coast, with a plethora of shopping centres, restaurants, discos, snack bars, amusement arcades and live entertainment aimed largely at the British and German tourist market.

Puerto de la Cruz

The beaches (see **BEACHES 1**) vary in quality but there are plenty of water-sports facilities, and just out of town is the Aguapark Octopus (see **CHILDREN**). This is a destination for those who like their holidays to be cheap and cheerful, and with plenty of unsophisticated nightlife. See **EXCURSION 1**.

Puerto de la Cruz: 39 km southwest of Santa Cruz. The most important resort on the north coast of Tenerife, it was founded in the 16thC as La Orotava's port and flourished through the trade in sugar and wine. In later years cochineal and bananas became the main commodities for export. Situated on the coast in front of the luxuriant banana plantations (see **A-Z**) of La Orotava valley, and with the magnificent Mount Teide (see **A-Z**) in the background, the town became a favourite winter resort for the British at the turn of the century and has since developed into a thriving yet dignified tourist resort. The old port retains much of its original character, in pleasant contrast to the new high-rise hotels and modern shops. There is much of historical interest in the town, including Casa Iriarte, Casa de la Real Aduana, and the 17thC church, Nuestra Señora de la Peña de Francia (see **ATTRACTIONS 3**). The Jardín Botánico (see **ATTRACTIONS 3**, **A-Z**) houses a unique collection of rare plants which thrive in the Canarian climate. An attractive 20thC development is the Lago de Martiánez (see **CHILDREN**), a designer lido which makes up for the resort's lack of good natural beaches (see **BEACHES** 2). See **NIGHTLIFE**, **RESTAURANTS 2**, **SHOPPING 2**, **WALK 2**.

Santa Cruz: 39 km northeast of Puerto de la Cruz. The modern-day capital of Tenerife and of the province which incorporates La Palma (see **A-Z**), Gomera (see **A-Z**) and Hierro (see **A-Z**), and site of the island's administrative institutions and military HQ. It has a population of 200,000, slightly less than Las Palmas, rival capital of the eastern province. One of Spain's biggest and most important ports, its main claim to historical fame is as the site of the battle of 1797 in which Horatio Nelson (see **A-Z**) lost his right arm and was forced to retreat. El Tigre, the cannon which fired the shot, is still preserved in the military museum at Castillo de Paso Alto (see **ATTRACTIONS** 1). In addition to its importance as a port, Santa Cruz is also a busy shopping centre. However, it still retains a colonial flavour, its housing being adorned with carved wooden balconies so typical of Canarian architecture. The centre of the city is dominated by the magnificent square, Plaza de España (see **WALK** 1), with its monument to the fallen of the Spanish Civil War (1936-39). Leading up from this is the Plaza de la Candelaria and the shopping precinct of c/ de Castillo, and beyond this lie the extensive grounds of the municipal park, Parque García Sanabria (see **ATTRACTIONS** 1). As befits a capital, Santa Cruz also contains some fine churches, as well as museums and an art gallery. In Feb. the city hosts a spectacular carnival (see **Events**). See **NIGHTLIFE 1**, **RESTAURANTS 1**, **SHOPPING 1**.

Santísimo Cristo de la Laguna: Brought to Tenerife by Alonso Fernández de Lugo (see **A-Z**) in 1520, this statue is housed in the 1513 Santuario del Cristo, a former Franciscan chapel (see **ATTRACTIONS 2**). It is a fine work of art, an ornate, black oak statue dating from the 15th-16thC and attributed to an anonymous artist of the Seville School. The Christ is displayed above the altar of the church in an embossed silver frame and is one of the island's most venerated pieces, the object of a pilgrimage every year on 14 Sep.

Playa de las Américas

Accidents & Breakdowns: If you are involved in a motoring accident, follow normal procedure by exchanging insurance details, names and addresses with the other party. Try to establish witnesses' details also. If someone is injured call the police (see **Emergency Numbers**). If you are driving your own car you will need a surety bond from your insurance company to exempt you from having to spend time in police custody while awaiting the outcome of any enquiry.

In case of breakdown, the Real Automóvil Club de Tenerife (the local equivalent of the RAC) offers reciprocal membership to drivers who subscribe to a club in their own country. Its office is on Avenida Anaga, Santa Cruz, tel: 270716. If you are driving a hired car, instructions on what to do in case of accident and breakdown should be printed on your contract. Garages are numerous throughout the island and generally provide a satisfactory service. If spare parts are not available for your make of car, long delays in completing repairs are inevitable. See **Consulates**, **Driving**.

Accommodation: In the high season it is essential to book a hotel prior to arrival as a large amount of the available accommodation consists of hotels which deal with travel firms offering package holidays. The same classification of hotels operates as on the mainland.

Paradores are luxurious, state-owned hotels. There is one on Tenerife, the Parador Nacional Las Cañadas del Teide (see **EXCURSION 2**), rated two-star. Although of moderate size, it has facilities such as a swimming pool, bar and tennis court. Tel: 232503.

Hotels range from five-star (luxurious) to one-star (comfortable but basic). Approximate prices for a double room during the high season are 20,000 ptas (five-star), 4500 ptas (three-star) and 3000 ptas (one-star). *Hostales* (H^s) are rated on a star system of one to three and generally provide much simpler accommodation.

A *fonda* (inn) is often good value, though usually found only in villages. On booking in you will be asked for your passport which will be returned to you the following morning. Self-catering, villa-style accommodation is also very popular and needs to be arranged prior to arrival. Time-share apartments and villas are also very much on the increase. See **Camping**, **Youth Hostels**.

Airports: Two airports serve Tenerife. The main international airport is at Reina Sofía to the south of the island, 65 km from Santa Cruz, tel: 770050. It handles regular flights to the mainland by several leading airlines and caters for numerous charter flights. You will also find the usual facilities, including car-hire agencies, a post office, a bureau de change, wheelchair facilities, information services, a self-service restaurant and a bookshop. Bus and taxi services operate between the airport and the main towns. A green TITSA bus to Santa Cruz costs 500 ptas and operates in conjunction with scheduled Air Iberia flights. A taxi to Santa Cruz will cost 5000-5500 ptas, and to Playa de las Américas or Los Cristianos about 2000 ptas.
The other airport is at Los Rodeos, near La Laguna, tel: 257940. It handles relatively inexpensive inter-island flights by Air Iberia. Bus services are available and a taxi to Santa Cruz will cost c. 1000 ptas.

Baby-sitters: The best way to find a reliable baby-sitter is to ask at your hotel. Two or three days' notice may be required during the high season and you can expect to pay 500 ptas per hr. See **CHILDREN**, **Children**.

Banks: See **Currency**, **Money**, **Opening Times**.

Best Buys: Santa Cruz is a free-trade port. There are no restrictions on the source of supply of articles, taxes are very low and there is no VAT. Therefore, an extremely wide range of cheap electrical goods, cameras, watches, perfume, jewellery and spirits is available. Furs are also inexpensive at about 40% less than elsewhere in Europe. Nevertheless, shoppers should be alert, as some apparent bargains may be goods of inferior quality. Local crafts include embroidery and lace, basketwork, pottery, wooden carvings and rugs. Cigars are also good value due to the availability of home-grown tobacco. See **SHOPPING 1 & 2**, **Markets**, **Shopping**.

Bicycle & Motorcycle Hire: Mopeds and motorcycles are a good way to see the island and it is possible to hire them at most beach resorts. For a Vespino the cost is c. 1000 ptas per day (reduced to 800 ptas daily for weekly hire). A Suzuki 750 would cost c. 2500 ptas per day. Insurance is an additional 300-500 ptas per day. Tenerife's roads vary greatly in quality and the volume of traffic carried, from remote and steep mountain tracks to fast main routes. Experience and caution are essential. Because of Tenerife's mountainous terrain and steep, winding roads, the hiring of bicycles is fairly uncommon and not really recommended for the casual cyclist.

Main hiring outlets:

Motos Santos – c/ Playa Azul, Playa de las Américas, tel: 791639.

Rosema – c/ de Méndez Núñez 49, Santa Cruz, tel: 480464.

Budget: 1992 prices. The cost of living is generally quite moderate in Tenerife, although self-catering holiday-makers should expect some grocery items to cost more than they may be used to.

Breakfast	600-700 ptas
Lunch	600-800 ptas (restaurant dish of the day)
Dinner	1500-3000 ptas
Wine	235 ptas (supermarket), 500 ptas (restaurant)
Soft drinks	200 ptas per litre
Museums	300-400 ptas

Buses: The main bus company on Tenerife is TITSA, tel: 215699 (Santa Cruz), 31807 (Puerto de la Cruz) or 795427 (Playa de las Américas). It operates an extensive and punctual service through most of the resorts and towns of the island. Buses are air-conditioned and clean. The main bus station in Santa Cruz is on Avenida Tres de Mayo, where you can reserve a seat for express services (generally only necessary at weekends when buses are crowded with families). Puerto de la Cruz bus station is situated on c/ del Pozo.

Cameras & Photography: Cameras are relatively cheap on Tenerife. Films are generally of reasonable quality, and there are plenty of 24 hr developing services. Make allowances for the strong sunlight, especially when taking pictures near whitewashed walls or the sand and sea. Some museums may allow photography. It is strictly forbidden to photograph any naval or military installation or personnel.

Camping: There is an official camp site at Nauta Camping, Cañada Blanca, Arona, tel: 785118. Basic charges start at 400 ptas per person for one night, with additional costs for cars, etc. It is well equipped, with a restaurant, shop, sports facilities and swimming pool, and is situated not far from the south coast beaches.

Car Hire: If you are travelling on a package holiday and know the type of car and number of days hire you need, it is usually cheaper to book in advance through your travel firm, or to contact Holiday Autos, a reliable broking firm, tel: 071-4911111. There are, however, many agencies in the main resorts and bigger towns, as well as at Reina Sofía (see **Airports**). Local agents are generally cheaper than the international companies but make sure that the contract you sign is in English and that comprehensive insurance is included. Minimum age is 23 when paying in cash, or 21 with a credit card. You will need either a national driving licence, issued at least one year previously, or an international driving permit.
Prices are about 2600 ptas per day for a Fiat Panda and 3000 ptas for a Renault 5, but insurance (1000 ptas per day) and a 4% tax are always added to the original quoted prices. See **Driving**.

Chemists: Chemists are easily identified by their green cross sign. Opening times (see **A-Z**) are the same as for other shops, with late opening determined by a rota system. Check in the window for the name and address of the nearest after-hours pharmacy. See **Health**.

Children: Children can readily be kept occupied in Tenerife and will enjoy the sea and sand and many of the available excursions. The Canarians love children and they will always be made welcome, even in restaurants and bars late at night. Many of the large hotels in the south have children's clubs to give parents a break, and apart from the beach there are birds and animals to see, go-karts and water slides to ride, and even camels for hire. See **CHILDREN**, **Baby-sitters**.

Climate: The Canary Islands enjoy a temperate climate all year round, with an average temperature of 16°C in Feb. and 24°C in Aug. On Tenerife the weather is affected by the mountains which separate the north and south coasts. The northern coast is often much cooler due to the *alisio* wind. In winter the southwestern coastal resorts are more likely to enjoy sunny weather. Due to the topography of Tenerife it is possible to experience the whole range of weather conditions when driving round the island, from sundrenched beaches to misty woodlands to the snowcapped peak of Mount Teide (see **A-Z**).

Complaints: The same system operates as on the Spanish mainland. Every hotel must keep a supply of *hojas de reclamaciones* (complaints forms), and often simply requesting one is sufficient to achieve results. If not, fill in the form in triplicate: one to retain, one for the tourist board and one for the establishment against which the complaint is being made. Such a procedure is treated very seriously and should not be abused. For major complaints involving violence or fraud, go directly to the police (see **A-Z**) or tourist office (see **Tourist Information**).

Consulates:
UK – Plaza Weyler 8, Santa Cruz, tel: 286863.
Republic of Ireland – Floor 6, c/ La Marina 7, Santa Cruz, tel: 245671.
USA – c/ Alvarez de Lugo 10, Santa Cruz, tel: 286950.

Conversion Chart:

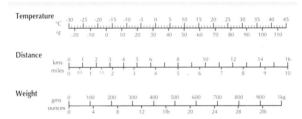

Temperature
°C -30 -25 -20 -15 -10 -5 0 5 10 15 20 25 30 35 40 45
°F -20 -10 0 10 20 30 40 50 60 70 80 90 100 110

Distance
kms 0 1 2 3 4 5 6 8 10 12 14 16
miles 0 0.5 1 1.5 2 3 4 5 6 7 8 9 10

Weight
gms 0 100 200 300 400 500 600 700 800 900 1kg
ounces 0 4 8 12 1lb 20 24 28 2lb

Crime & Theft: Certain simple precautions can be taken to help prevent a theft from spoiling your holiday: leave all valuables in the hotel safe; don't carry large amounts of cash around with you; don't take valuables to the beach; leave the car in an official car park which has an attendant; don't leave anything of value in the car as thefts from hire cars are very common; if your room has a balcony, remember to close the windows before going out. If you are robbed, you should inform the hotel at once and they will contact the police (see **A-Z**). In case of theft in the street, go to the police who will help you make the necessary statement for any insurance claim. If you have financial

problems or lose your passport, you should also contact your consulate
(see **A-Z**). See **Emergency Numbers**, **Insurance**.

Currency: The Spanish unit of currency is the peseta (pta).
Coins – 1, 5, 10, 25, 50, 100, 200, 500 ptas.
Notes – 100, 500, 1000, 2000, 5000 ptas.

Customs Allowances:

UK/EC	Cigarettes	Cigarillos	Cigars	Tobacco	Still Table Wine	Spirits/Liqueurs	Fortified Wine	Additional Still Table Wine	Perfume	Toilet Water	Gifts & Souvenirs
Duty Free	200	100	50	250 g	2 l	1 l	2 l	2 l	60 cc/ml	250 cc/ml	£32
Duty Paid	800	400	200	1 kg	90 l*	10 l	20 l				

* Of which no more than 60 l should be sparkling wine.

Since 1 Jan. 1993 restrictions on allowances for duty-paid goods
brought into the UK from any EC country have been abolished.
Travellers are now able to buy goods, including alcoholic drinks and
tobacco, paying duty and VAT in the EC country where the goods are
purchased. However, duty-paid goods should be for the traveller's own
use and carried by him personally. Whereas previously there were
either-or options, travellers can now bring back the sum of the goods in
the duty-paid column.

Disabled People: Provision is made for wheelchair travellers in
many parts of Tenerife. Reina Sofía (see **Airports**) has facilities for the
disabled, and resorts such as Playa de las Américas and Los Cristianos
have ramps giving access to restaurants, etc. See **Health**, **Insurance**.

Drinks: Locally-produced drinks include *ron* (white rum), liqueurs made from coffee, orange and bananas, and wines which, although hard to find in tourist areas, offer a pleasant accompaniment to a meal in village inns. Don't be surprised if your wine is served in a soft drink bottle, as this means that it has been drawn straight from the barrel. The most famous wine is *malvasía* or malmsey. Typical Spanish drinks found on the island include *sangría* (an often potent mixture of wine, orange juice and spirits, decorated with fruit), *jerez* or sherry (the three main varieties being a dry fino and a medium amontillado for apéritifs, and a sweet oloroso to accompany desserts) and the local brandy or *coñac* (rougher than its French counterpart). *Cerveza* or beer is both locally-produced and imported from the mainland.

Driving: If you decide to take your own car to Tenerife, you'll need your driving licence (preferably an international driving permit), green card insurance, bail bond (also from your insurance company) and the vehicle registration document. You must wear your seat belt when driving outside of main towns, and young children (under 10) must not travel in the front seats. The quality of the roads varies greatly, and care is required at all times. Beware of large and unexpected potholes and unmarked sharp bends on mountain roads. Progress in these mountain areas can be very slow so allow more time than usual for whatever distance you have to travel. Let local traffic pass when it is safe to do so. There are two stretches of motorway on the island: Santa Cruz to Puerto de la Cruz (Autopista del Norte) and Santa Cruz to Reina Sofía airport (Autopista del Sur). In general, on the island the road markings and signposting are often inadequate, and it is easy to miss turnings. As it is not easy to obtain good maps on Tenerife, it is recommended that you buy a suitable map in the UK. Stanford's, Long Acre, Covent Garden, London, tel: 071-8361321, have a mail-order service. Stick to main roads, as tracks which seem to be in good condition can quickly deteriorate. Towns can often be busy and congested so take care. The speed limit in towns is 40 kph, on other main roads 90 kph, and on motorways 120 kph. Crash helmets must be worn on motorcycles. The Guardia Civil and Policía Municipal deal with traffic offenders (see **Police**). See **Accidents & Breakdowns**, **Parking**, **Petrol**.

Drugs: Possession of small amounts of both soft and hard drugs for personal use remains legal within the Canary Islands but as amounts are not defined by law, possession of any drugs is a high risk. Trading in drugs is illegal and there are severe penalties for offenders. Despite this, you may be approached in the street in the more popular resorts. Contact your consulate (see **A-Z**) if you are arrested for a drugs-related offence.

Eating Out: For authentic Canarian cooking leave the buffet meals served in hotels and try one of the many restaurants around the island. In Santa Cruz and Puerto de la Cruz it is possible to sample a wide variety of different dishes, and the establishments in the smaller towns usually provide a good choice of local cuisine. Grading of restaurants works on a 'fork' system, five forks signifying a high standard of facilities though not necessarily the best value food. It is best to follow the example of the locals in looking for good food, regardless of the décor of the establishment. A service charge is often included in your bill but you may wish to leave a 5-10% tip if you are particularly satisfied with your meal and the service. The bigger towns have adapted to the demands of tourists and start serving in the evening at 1900 or 2000, but in the smaller villages it is still customary to eat later, at about 2200. Approximate price ranges for a three-course dinner (exc. drinks) are 1000-1500 ptas (Inexpensive), 1500-3000 ptas (Moderate) and 3000-6000 ptas (Expensive). See **RESTAURANTS 1-4**, **Food**.

Electricity: Mainly 220V with round-pin, two-point plugs, so that adaptors are normally required for UK appliances. These are available in most large supermarkets at about 400 ptas.

Emergency Numbers:

Police	091
Fire	220080 (Santa Cruz)
	330080 (Puerto de la Cruz)
Ambulance	281800 (Santa Cruz)
	383812 (Puerto de la Cruz)
	790505 (Los Cristianos)

| Emergency medical services | 710620 (Playa de las Américas)
241502 (Santa Cruz)
383812 (Puerto de la Cruz) |

Events: There are numerous festivals in Tenerife throughout the year. Some of the more colourful and popular ones include:

5-6 January: Cabalgata de los Reyes Magos (Procession of the Three Kings) at Santa Cruz.

February: Carnival starts six weeks before Lent and is preceded by the election of the carnival queen. There follow two weeks of dancing in the streets, music and costumed processions in Santa Cruz, Puerto de la Cruz and other parts of the island.

March: Holy Week parades, especially interesting at La Laguna and Santa Cruz.

May & June: Corpus Christi processions, particularly in La Orotava and La Laguna, where marvellous carpets are made out of flowers and sand.

June: The Romería de San Isidro, a costumed pilgrimage from San Isidro to La Orotava, with carts drawn by bullocks; *24:* Fiesta de San Juan at Icod de los Vinos.

July: Fiesta del Mar, a combination of secular water sports and religious

ceremonies at Santa Cruz and Puerto de la Cruz; *1st Sun. in July:*
Romería de San Benito Abad, a costumed parade with ox-drawn carts
at La Laguna; *16:* Fiesta de la Virgen del Carmen at Santa Cruz.
15 August: Romería de la Virgen de la Candelaria, where the appear-
ance of the Virgin to the Guanches (see **A-Z**) is re-enacted. See **Nuestra
Señora de la Candelaria**.
September: Fiestas del Santísimo Cristo. Processions, drama, sport, cultural displays and poetry readings at La Laguna and Tacoronte.
See **Music**.

Food: Apart from the familiar Spanish dishes such as paella, you will
also find food more typical of the Canary Islands:
Gofio – Dating from Guanche (see **A-Z**) times, a mixture of roasted
corn or oat flour with water, and added to sauces or served as an
accompaniment to various dishes.
Puchero – A dish resembling the French pot-au-feu; vegetables stewed
with meat, usually pork or veal.
Sancocho – Salted fish and sweet potatoes stew.
Conejo en salmorejo – Rabbit served in a spicy sauce.
Mojo picón – A tangy, red-hot sauce accompanying fish or meat.
Mojo verde – A herb sauce.
Fresh fish, whether fried, grilled or boiled, is on nearly every menu.
Sole and tuna are popular, and the local favourites include *vieja, corv-
ina* and *cherne*. Also worth trying is the delicious and distinctive goat's
milk cheese, another local product.
Tapas are small portions of food such as mountain-cured ham (*jamon
serrano*), cheese, olives, meatballs, seafood salads, Spanish omelette
(*tortilla*), etc. They are available on the counter in many bars and are an
excellent and informal way of sampling several different dishes. Beware
though: the cost of several *tapas* dishes can soon mount up to more
than an ordinary meal. See RESTAURANTS 1-4, **Eating Out**.

Health: Before leaving for Tenerife, EC residents can obtain form E111
entitling them to free medical attention while on holiday. It is also
advisable to take out health insurance while booking your holiday to
cover the expense of treatment and emergency travel home.

General Hospital – Carretera del Norte (between Santa Cruz and La
Laguna), tel: 641011/646312.
Hospital Las Américas – Adjacent to Guardia Civil, Los Cristianos,
tel: 750022.
Children's Hospital – c/ Carmen Monteverde 47, Santa Cruz,
tel: 286550.
Hospital Tamaragna – c/ Agustín de Bethencourt, Puerto de la Cruz,
tel: 380512.
Most doctors speak some English. The most common medical problems
experienced by tourists are brought on by an excess of food, drink and
exposure to the sun, so moderation is advised if you don't want to spoil
your holiday. Also be prepared for variations in weather conditions
when travelling around the island, especially if walking. See **Chemists**,
Disabled People.

Insurance: You should take out travel insurance covering you against
theft and loss of property and money, as well as medical expenses, for
the duration of your stay. Your travel agent should be able to recom-
mend a suitable policy. See **Crime & Theft**, **Driving**, **Health**.

Laundries: Hotels have laundries and dry-cleaning services, though
they are likely to be relatively expensive. In the southern resorts there
are Launderettes at Pueblo Canario, Playa de las Américas and next to
Hermusa at the entrance to Los Cristianos.

Lost Property: There is no lost-property office on the island. If the
loss is serious, report it to the Policía Nacional (see **Police**) but do not
hold out any hope of recovery. Promptly advise any credit card companies, issuers of traveller's cheques and, if your passport is lost, your consulate (see **A-Z**). See **Insurance**.

Markets: The big fruit and vegetable market in Santa Cruz is called
Nuestra Señora de África (see ATTRACTIONS 1). It offers colourful displays
of local produce, with fish on sale in the basement. Most villages also
have their own market day. There is a crafts and flea market at La
Orotava every Sat. on the terrace above the bus station.

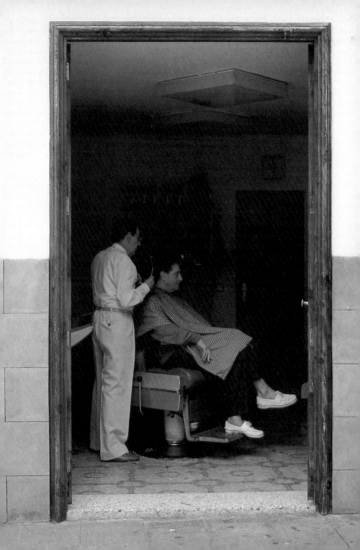

Money: There are numerous bureaux de change which keep roughly the same opening times (see **A-Z**) as shops. Banks are plentiful in the major towns and offer all the customary services. Many of them charge a minimum commission of 400-500 ptas when changing currency or traveller's cheques. Hotels offer the same rate of exchange for money as banks.

Eurocheques are normally accepted in the larger establishments, as are all major credit cards. If your card is lost or stolen, tel: 91-4599009 (American Express) or 91-4352445 (Visa and Mastercard). Many hotels will exchange traveller's cheques but they offer less favourable terms than banks. You will require your passport for transactions concerning traveller's cheques.

Music: Tenerife has its own symphony orchestra. The season is Oct.-April, with concerts in the Parque San Francisco in Puerto de la Cruz. For tickets and information about concerts, contact Oficinas del Parque San Francisco, c/ Agustín de Bethencourt, Puerto de la Cruz, tel: 383620. The music festival takes place in Jan. and lasts for one month, with concerts at the Teatro Guimero in Santa Cruz and the university in La Laguna. For information, contact Patronata Insular de Música, Cabildo de Tenerife, Plaza de España 1, Santa Cruz, tel: 242090. Canary Island folk music, with its Spanish and Latin American

influences, mixes lively songs and dances with slower melodies. Groups such as the Taburiente, Los Majuelos and the Sabandeños have led a revival in traditional music, and the Canaries have their own unique musical creation, the small stringed instrument known as the *timple*.

Newspapers: Many foreign newspapers are on sale in the main towns and resorts the day after publication. Apart from the regional Spanish papers, there is also the *Diario de Avisos*, a daily newspaper with an English and German edition every two weeks. See **What's On**.

Opening Times: These vary greatly, but generally:
Shops – 0900/0930-1300, 1600/1630-1930 Mon.-Sat. (winter) and 0900/0930-1300, 1700-2000 Mon.-Sat. (summer).
Banks – 0900-1400 Mon.-Fri., 0900-1300 Sat. Closed Sat., June-Aug.
Post offices – 0800/0900-1400/1500 Mon.-Fri., 0900-1300 Sat.
Museums – 0900/1000-1300, 1500/1600-1800/1900 Mon.-Sat., but times vary according to the season, presentation of temporary exhibitions, etc. Tourist offices (see **Tourist Information**) may be able to help with specific enquiries.
Churches – 0900-1200, 1700-2000 Mon.-Sat. Again though, there are no set hours. See **Religious Services**.

Orientation: Tenerife is the largest island in the Canary Islands (see **A-Z**), an archipelago of seven islands lying just off the west coast of Africa. It has a distinctive three-cornered shape, with the Punta de Anaga in the northeast, the Punta de Teno in the northwest, and the Punta de la Rasca in the south, forming the three protruding angles. The island is divided along a northeast–southwest axis by a series of mountain ranges, starting with the Anaga mountains (see **A-Z**) in the northwest, increasing in altitude to Mount Teide (see **A-Z**) in the centre (3717 m), and then on to the Teno mountains on the southwest coast. The capital of Tenerife, Santa Cruz (see **A-Z**), lies on the southern slopes of the Anaga massif. There are few rivers on the island, due to the sharp inclination of the mountains and their proximity to the coast. See **ISLANDS**.

Parking: This can be extremely difficult in the bigger resorts and towns, and it is often wise to leave your car with an attendant, despite the small extra cost. The international sign (white 'P' on a blue background) indicates official car parks. It is an offence to park facing the traffic. See **Driving**.

Petrol: This is cheap (about 65 ptas per litre or 295 ptas per gallon), and there are petrol stations in most villages and along the main roads. Outside the larger resorts and towns you may find that filling stations close during the evenings and all day Sun. See **Driving**.

Police: There are three types of police in Spain:
The Guardia Civil wear a dark green uniform. They are responsible for offences concerning national security, e.g. border control, and also serve as traffic police outside towns.
Santa Cruz, tel: 223100; Puerto de la Cruz, tel: 33528.
The Policía Municipal wear navy blue uniforms and deal with local problems and traffic control within towns.
Santa Cruz, tel: 092; Puerto de la Cruz, tel: 380428.
The Policía Nacional deal with serious crimes, e.g. drugs and theft.
Santa Cruz, tel: 091; Puerto de la Cruz, tel: 381224.
See **Crime & Theft**, **Emergency Numbers**.

Post Offices: Post offices only deal with letters, parcels and tele-grams – the telephone system is separate (see **Telephones & Telegrams**). Stamps can be purchased in tobacconists and in most places which sell postcards. It costs 45 ptas to send a postcard or letter weighing less than 20 g. See **Opening Times**.

Public Holidays:
1 Jan. (New Year's Day); 6 Jan. (Epiphany); 19 Mar. (St. Joseph's Day); Easter (movable feast); 1 May (Labour Day); July (Corpus Christi); 25 July (St. James' Day); 15 Aug. (Assumption); 12 Oct. (Discovery of America); 1 Nov. (All Saints' Day); 8 Dec. (Immaculate Conception); 25 Dec. (Christmas Day). In addition to these general public holidays there are local holidays, festivals and celebrations. See **Events**.

Rabies: Still exists here as in other parts of the Continent. As a pre-caution, have all animal bites seen to by a doctor.

Religious Services:
All Saints' Anglican Church – Parque Taoro, Puerto de la Cruz. 0930

Sun. (1100 1st and 3rd Sun. of each month) and 1000 Wed.
Evangelical Church – c/ Iriarte 6, Puerto de la Cruz. 1000 Sun.
Nuestra Señora de la Peña de Francía – Plaza de la Iglesia, Puerto de la
Cruz. International Mass, mostly in English, 1000 Sun.
Nuestra Señora de Guadalupe – Playa de las Américas. Roman
Catholic Mass in English, 1000 Sun.
Hotel Andreas – Los Cristianos. Evangelical service, 1100 Sun.

Shopping: The best place to
shop for items benefitting from
the low tax system is Santa
Cruz. There is a multitude of
shops and bazaars along c/ de
Castillo. These are often run
by Indians who speak English,
Spanish and German. Always
check quality and guarantees
before making a purchase. It is
wise to go to one of the big
department stores first to get
an idea of what is available.
Bargaining can be an accept-
able practice in the smaller
shops where prices are not
marked. A choice of craftwork
is available in both Santa Cruz
and Puerto de la Cruz, though
it is often more interesting to
buy pieces from the smaller
villages. Puerto de la Cruz is
also noted for its choice of furs

at reasonable prices. As is often the case on islands, everyday household goods, food and clothes often have to be imported and can therefore be expensive. There are numerous supermarkets on the island,
with small variations in prices, but it is also fun to try shopping for food
at the market in Santa Cruz. See **SHOPPING 1 & 2**, **Best Buys**, **Markets**.

Smoking: Tenerife is a smoker's haven as cigarettes and cigars are cheap and there are few public restrictions on smoking. As the island is duty-free, the allocation of cigarettes for returning holiday-makers remains at 200 per person, even if you have purchased the goods on the island. See **Customs Allowances**.

Sports: A variety of participatory and spectator sports can be enjoyed on Tenerife. For the energetic, there are numerous tennis courts as well as horse riding centres and golf courses, and the countryside affords many enjoyable walks (see **Walking**). Most sporting activity is based around the sea, however. If you are interested in more than just swimming, the main resorts also provide facilities for diving, sailing, windsurfing, water-skiing, jet-skiing or fishing.
Of the local spectator sports, soccer is the big favourite with the islanders, and most towns have a playing field. The main stadium is the Estadio H. Rodríguez López, off c/ San Sebastián in Santa Cruz, where Tenerife play in the Spanish first division. Canarian wrestling (see **A-Z**) is also of interest.

Taxis: Taxis can be identified by a green light at night or a green *libre* sign displayed on windscreens during the day. The flag-down charge is 55 ptas and the journey is charged at 30 ptas per km. It costs 650 ptas per hr to ask a taxi to wait for you. Not all taxis are metered and it is best to negotiate a price in advance for excursions or longer trips. See **Tipping**.

Telephones & Telegrams: Telephone boxes are plentiful and those marked 'Internacional' can be used to telephone abroad. They take 5, 25, 50 and 100 pta coins, and clear instructions in English, French and German are provided. To telephone abroad, first dial 07 and, when you hear a change in the dialling tone, enter the appropriate international code (e.g. UK – 44, USA – 01). Then dial the area code (without the initial 0) and the rest of the number. There are also very convenient Teléfonico public telephone offices, identified by the sign of a blue telephone, where the fee is paid at the desk after the call is made. Charges are the same. Hotels, however, usually levy a hefty surcharge on telephone calls. Telegrams can be sent either by telephone or through the post office (see **A-Z**), which in Santa Cruz also has fax and telex facilities. See **Emergency Numbers**.

Television & Radio: The Canary Island tourist radio station broadcasts in English from Las Palmas on MW 747 khz, Mon.-Sat. Local Spanish radio stations include Radio Club Tenerife, Radio Cadine, Radio Español and Antenna Tres. The two Spanish TV channels can also be received, with local variations. Occasionally they show foreign films with their original soundtracks, usually late at night. Several of the bars and cafés in modern resorts such as Playa de las Américas show video programmes in English.

Time Difference: The same as Greenwich Mean Time.

Tipping: While tipping is not always necessary (a service charge is normally included in bills), it is becoming customary. If you are happy with the service, leave approximately 10% for taxi drivers, waiters and guides (or 200 ptas for the latter), c. 100 ptas per bag for the hotel porter and 200 ptas per week for the hotel maid.

Toilets: There are few public toilets on the island. You may go into a bar or café and ask for *servicios*, though you are expected to buy something such as a glass of wine or cup of coffee, out of courtesy.

Tourist Information: In Santa Cruz there are two tourist offices offering friendly advice from staff fluent in English, French and German. Maps, brochures and free posters are available. Tenerife is still in the process of developing its tourist industry and this is reflected in the fact that some events are poorly publicized, tourist office opening times are erratic, and even tourist office staff may be unaware of attractions' opening times, prices, etc.
Tourist offices:
Santa Cruz – Palacio Insular, Plaza de España, tel: 242593. 0800-1500 Mon.-Fri., 0900-1300 Sat.
Santa Cruz – c/ La Marina 57, tel: 283853. 0800-1500.
Puerto de la Cruz – Plaza de la Iglesia 3, tel: 386000. 0800-1400.

Lago de Martiánez

Tours: Organized coach trips to all parts of Tenerife are readily available, departing from the main towns. The most popular tours include Mount Teide (see **A-Z**), the Anaga mountains (see **A-Z**), the shops of Santa Cruz (see **SHOPPING 1**), and nightspots such as the exotic La Cueva (see **NIGHTLIFE**) and the ever-popular Medieval Night, from Playa de las Américas and Los Cristianos. The Donkey Safari from Arafo is a more unusual treat. The coastal towns provide a choice of boat trips, short excursions around Tenerife itself, and longer cruises to the other islands. Air travel within the Canaries is relatively inexpensive, and a day trip to La Palma (see **A-Z**) or Gran Canaria (see **A-Z**) is feasible on a moderate budget. The coast of North Africa is also within reach of Gran Canaria.

Transport: There are no trains on Tenerife but the bus services are generally good, although the roads themselves vary in quality in the rural districts. Boats also provide occasional links between the major resorts. Transport between the islands is relatively inexpensive by air, a good alternative to the fairly long ferry journeys if time is limited. The 80 min hydrofoil trip from Santa Cruz to Las Palmas on Gran Canaria (see **A-Z**) is a special attraction. See **Airports**, **Buses**, **Taxis**.

Traveller's Cheques: See **Money**.

Walking: Among the best of the many regions of Tenerife which offer marvellous countryside for walking are the Parque Nacional del Teide (see **A-Z**), the Anaga mountains (see **A-Z**) and the Teno mountain range (see **EXCURSION 1**). A gentler walk is to be found along the Barranco del Infierno (see **A-Z**). Walkers should take care to equip themselves properly to cope with the often rough terrain and the variable climate at higher altitudes. See **WALKS 1-4**.

What's On: There are two monthly magazines printed mainly for British residents on the island but also containing useful information about local events, eating out, where to go and what to do. They are the *Island Gazette* (220 ptas) and *Tenerife Today* (200 ptas), both available from international bookshops and some kiosks. See **Events**, **Newspapers**.

Youth Hostels: There are no youth hostels on Tenerife. The cheapest alternative accommodation is camping (see **A-Z**).

This edition published 1995 by Diamond Books
77–85 Fulham Palace Road
Hammersmith, London W6 8JB

Text: William Coffey
Photography: James Carney
Electronic Cartography: Susan Harvey Design

First published 1990 Second edition 1993
Copyright © HarperCollins*Publishers*

Printed in Italy

ISBN 0 261 66595-2